The Value of Money

Uncover the Hidden Wisdom of Money

Susan McCarthy

Jeremy P. Tarcher/Penguin
a member of Penguin Group (USA) Inc.
New York

JEREMY P. TARCHER/PENGUIN
Published by the Penguin Group
Penguin Group (USA) Inc., 375 Hudson Street, New York, New York 10014, USA • Penguin Group
(Canada), 90 Eglinton Avenue East, Suite 700, Toronto, Ontario M4P 2Y3, Canada (a division
of Pearson Canada Inc.) • Penguin Books Ltd, 80 Strand, London WC2R 0RL, England • Penguin
Ireland, 25 St Stephen's Green, Dublin 2, Ireland (a division of Penguin Books Ltd) • Penguin Group
(Australia), 250 Camberwell Road, Camberwell, Victoria 3124, Australia (a division of Pearson
Australia Group Pty Ltd) • Penguin Books India Pvt Ltd, 11 Community Centre, Panchsheel Park,
New Delhi–110 017, India • Penguin Group (NZ), 67 Apollo Drive, Rosedale, North Shore 0632,
New Zealand (a division of Pearson New Zealand Ltd) • Penguin Books (South Africa) (Pty) Ltd,
24 Sturdee Avenue, Rosebank, Johannesburg 2196, South Africa

Penguin Books Ltd, Registered Offices: 80 Strand, London WC2R 0RL, England

Most Tarcher/Penguin books are available at special quantity discounts for bulk purchase
for sales promotions, premiums, fund-raising, and educational needs. Special books or book
excerpts also can be created to fit specific needs. For details, write Penguin Group (USA) Inc.
Special Markets, 375 Hudson Street, New York, NY 10014.

Library of Congress Cataloging-in-Publication Data

McCarthy, Susan.
    The value of money : uncover the hidden wisdom of money / Susan McCarthy.
        p.   cm.
    Includes index.
    ISBN 978-1-58542-644-7
    1. Finance, Personal.   2. Money.   I. Title.
    HG179.M37423   2008   2008006673
    332.024—dc22

Printed in the United States of America
10   9   8   7   6   5   4   3   2   1

Book design by Meighan Cavanaugh

This publication is designed to provide accurate and authoritative information in regard to the subject
matter covered. It is sold with the understanding that the publisher is not engaged in rendering legal,
accounting, or other professional services. If you require legal advice or other expert assistance, you
should seek the services of a competent professional.

While the author has made every effort to provide accurate telephone numbers and Internet addresses at
the time of publication, neither the publisher nor the author assumes any responsibility for errors, or for
changes that occur after publication. Further, the publisher does not have any control over and does not
assume any responsibility for author or third-party websites or their content.

To Veronica and Michael,
the loves of my life

CONTENTS

AUTHOR'S NOTE

In the business of handling other people's money, confidentiality is of extreme importance. The stories told in this book, as well as the characters that play roles in them, are composites drawn from the lives of many different clients with whom I've worked. Although I have, of course, concealed the identity of my clients, and thus fictionalized specific details of their stories, I have not concealed the tone nor true nature of our work together.

Wachovia Corporation and its entities are not liable or responsible for any and all information contained in this book. Opinions expressed are solely those of the author.

This book offers general information regarding personal, financial, and retirement planning. It cannot address all specific individual situations and therefore is not intended as financial advice. Consult with a qualified adviser regarding your specific situation.

It is not the intent of the author to offer tax advice. Consult with a qualified tax adviser regarding your specific situation.

It is not the intent of the author to offer estate-planning advice. Consult with a qualified estate planner/legal expert regarding your specific situation.

With all investments or investment strategies discussed in this book, past performance is not a guarantee of future results.

I.

The Potential
of Money

Wall Street was the last place I ever expected to find grace. It wasn't a spiritual path that I had in mind when I began my work as a financial adviser. But here in the midst of stocks and bonds, PE ratios, competition, and money, money, money, I have discovered a world of deep human connection and a vast opportunity for personal growth. What I have learned is that the world of money is one of emotion, a stage on which we play out all of our dramas and, as such, that it can be an unexpected source of spiritual lessons. Most of us think of greed and jealousy at the mention of money and emotion, but there is as much room for compassion and grace in the world of money as there is in any aspect of our lives.

For over two decades I have served as a financial adviser with two major global financial services firms. My clients include institutions, families, and individuals, with different goals and varying needs. I work with money that must care for the poor, educate the young, secure retirements, run organizations, provide income, or simply grow. And, like all serious financial advisers, I work with complicated financial strategies as well as with capital markets from around the world. I am the liaison between my clients and their investments, the face of Wall Street for those whom I serve.

This all sounds quite grand. Indeed, it's this sophisticated, business-oriented view of our work that most financial advisers like to hold. And, for the most part, it's true. But there's another side to this world of money and investments, a side that is tangled up with human emotion. It's the side that involves the intricacies of the investments less than the intricacies of the investors themselves and especially investors in the midst of financial decision making: the ways, for example, in which fear can be a greater stumbling block to financial success than anything going on in the markets. Or the ways in which a person filled with anger can use money as a powerful weapon. Or the ways in which a self-destructive person can use money to sabotage him or herself. I've been both surprised and gratified by the number of times I've been involved with my clients as they work out some of the common but thorny emotional issues that life and money together present. This is a side of money management that is never far from the surface and that affects every part of life. It's an aspect of the money business too long ignored by those who advise people on financial decisions, but it's well known to all who make them.

The Dilemma of Putting the Emotion Back into Money Management

From the outside, the world of money seems to be a mixture of complicated strategies, global influences, power brokers, and dumb luck. The investment world presents a dizzying array of choices. From the outside, there often appears to be little consensus on the direction of the markets among those who purport to know, often leaving investors confused by conflicting advice. It's no wonder that many people are nervous when faced with major financial decisions or just investing in general.

There's far more involved in managing money, however, than what fills the financial news each day. For most of us, dealing with our money, especially making decisions at important junctures in our lives, is an unexpected tangle of the highly quantifiable and the purely subjective. Making financial decisions and managing our money are as much about understanding our fears, strengths, and weaknesses as about understanding how investments work. Beneath the quantitative, masculine, and analytical skin of money management, there beats a heart of raw emotion.

I believe that most of us understand this on some level. We know that our relationship to money is emotional. If you've ever had to make any one of a number of major financial decisions—investing retirement money, taking over the care of an elderly parent, receiving an inheritance, to name just three—you know that your decisions can be governed as much by knee-jerk emotional reactions as by any financial concerns or market conditions. The truth is that money and emotion go hand in hand.

Many people in the investment world feel that in order to be financially successful we must set aside our emotions. But I disagree. I believe you must acknowledge your emotions and study how they relate to your money. To make the best possible financial decisions, you must understand your relationship to money. There's great power in this understanding, great potential for freedom and growth. It's a simple tool, this money, but it's everywhere in our lives, a current that flows through every relationship we have, many of the decisions we make, and every generation. It may be a simple tool, but it's also one of our most accessible and powerful tools for growth and change. The challenge is to see it as such.

How I Learned That Money and Emotion Are Inextricably Linked

In my early years of working with people and their money, I was mostly concerned with building a practice and learning all I could about the intricacies of investing. My focus was on money because, of course, that was where I believed it needed to be. I perceived my most important contribution to my clients' lives to be my knowledge of investments and how to apply them to an individual's personal situation. And, of course, that's still my responsibility. It's still what people come to me for and a responsibility I take very seriously.

But on one extraordinary day, I was given an unusual opportunity to glimpse a more important aspect of my work. This was the day my eyes were opened to the real key to understanding money and to the huge potential that this understanding could offer. We've all experienced those odd "coincidences" in life that prove to be important turning points. Mine came on that one day in an odd juxtaposition of client situations that was so striking, I could hardly miss it.

It began on the day before Thanksgiving many years ago. One of my favorite clients called me early in the morning at home and, with great excitement in his voice, asked me to meet him at the office as soon as possible. He had recently negotiated the sale of his business. After what must have felt like years to him, he was, at last, holding a check for several million dollars.

We met in my office first thing of course. The mood was decidedly festive. This payment was the culmination of his business life, a life filled with devotion, hard work, creativity, and hundreds of ups and downs. Here was the reward larger than most, that so many people dream of. It was a symbol of his success as well as a guarantee of his future financial security. He was proud, excited, and a little scared to be entering the new phase of life that this check afforded him, that retirement phase that so many of us wish for but secretly fear. He and I set about implementing the investment strategy that we had already discussed at length.

As he was leaving my office that afternoon, he asked if I would call a friend of his who was working for a small company that was being bought out by another. The new owners were terminating the old retirement plan, and so all employees were to receive their money directly in what's called a "lump-sum distribution." My client mentioned that his friend had a number of questions about this process, one that can be rather complicated. He also mentioned in passing that she was quite nervous about it. I promised to call before I left that day.

When I reached her later that afternoon, I was shocked. "Quite nervous" barely described what this poor woman was feeling. In all my years of dealing with people and their money, I had never seen anyone more anxious about receiving some. Many people would have been excited about this distribution, but not this woman. She was petrified!

I quickly realized as she spoke that, although she was very apprehensive about this retirement plan distribution, the money wasn't really the issue at all. For her, too, this money was a symbol but not one of success. This retirement plan distribution had come to represent all the fears she had about her future: her company, her job, and her security. For her, this money was a symbol of uncertainty and change, and she hated change.

In truth, her anxiety was easy to understand. She and all her fellow employees found themselves in a very ambiguous situation, one that's quite common in today's workplace: Their company had changed hands. No one knew exactly what job they would have when the dust settled or even if they would have a job; it was easy for them to fear the worst. For this woman, being asked to take over the management of her own retirement plan money represented an unwelcome task in an uncertain situation. It represented the loss of leadership and order, the first step in her being cut loose.

After a long phone conversation with her (in which at least I was able to answer several of her questions), I headed home. My mind was filled with thoughts about these two quite different situations. It did strike me as an odd coincidence that I had met with these two individuals on the same day. They were both taking control of significant amounts of money, but their attitudes couldn't have been more different. We certainly were running the gamut of emotions here! But my eye-opening day was not quite complete. There was more to come.

Before I'd even made it home, I received a call from my assistant, who told me with great urgency that I needed to contact a client immediately. This client, Jean, and her husband, Walt, were new clients who had just retired. They were young for retirement—still in their fifties—and they had lots of plans for their new life. Unlike many who regard retirement with fear and trepidation, these two had approached it with great gusto. But that very morning, Walt had been killed in an auto accident. I pulled my own car off the road and called.

Of course Jean was beside herself with the torrent of emotions that accompanies this kind of tragedy. Shock, fear, anger, sorrow, pain—it was all there in her voice. We spoke of him, of his death, of what she was trying to do with herself that day. Finally we got to the money. She had received a call from a friend who was also a financial adviser, asking her to make some decisions regarding some money that her husband had. I'd like to believe that this gentleman was trying to help. When there's been a death, we all look for ways to reach out to the people most affected. I imagine he was trying to make himself useful, but on that day Jean was barely able to decide what shoes to put on, let alone what to do with her money. She was such a kind and gentle person that I was surprised when she shouted into the phone, "Susan, I don't want to think about this stuff!! Handle it for me!" She slammed down the receiver.

That evening, with a bit of time to reflect, I realized how important this day had been. Here were three radically different situations. For my first client, who had sold his business, the situation was filled with joy, excitement, and pride. For his friend, a fairly straightforward payment out of her retirement plan had come to represent a crisis in her work life. And Jean, of course, was facing one of life's most difficult and stressful of all situations, the loss of her spouse. These were three major transitions in the lives of these three individuals.

I began to think about all the changes I had witnessed in my clients' lives—births, deaths, retirements, inheritances, sending children off to college, welcoming them back home, taking over for the elderly, buying and selling businesses, settling estates— and I realized how much I had been conditioned as a professional financial adviser to wait quietly for the emotions to subside before advising my clients. What I really wanted to do, however, was allow them to acknowledge how closely bound their emotions and their money actually were and to permit this awareness to inform their next financial moves.

The Truth About Money

On this one extraordinary day, I realized a number of things. I realized first of all how incredibly privileged I was to be able to help people at these important transitions in their lives, how lucky I was to be trusted in this way. I also realized, however, that financial decisions are not necessarily difficult in and of themselves. It's our emotions that make them hard. Money and emotion are forever intertwined and never more so than when we're dealing with the financial ramifications of some life event or major change.

On this day I also began to grasp what has become for me personally perhaps the most important lesson of my work: A deep understanding of the intricate relationship between money and emotion can pave the way for not just greater financial success but personal and spiritual growth as well. This is possible, however, only if we allow ourselves to acknowledge what our emotions are telling us, if we recognize what we truly want and need from our money and act accordingly. After all, as I have said before and will most likely say again many times to come, money is simply a tool. It truly is *just* a currency we can use to achieve happiness and satisfaction in our lives. Why then should we try to separate it from our innermost needs and feelings? We should not, and, I would add, we most likely cannot. In *The Value of Money* you will learn how to recognize and understand the deep and often unconscious emotions that surround your money. And you will discover how you can use this newfound self-awareness not just to manage your money with greater ease but also to use money to expand, improve, and free yourself.

My Hope for You

In *The Value of Money* we will examine the complicated relationships we all have with our money. In Part I, we will explore the seven most common "money types" I have seen over the years and determine what type or combination of types you might be. We will also explore together the five most significant spiritual lessons that working with money has afforded me. I hope that these two aspects of this book will become tools you can use to better understand yourself and the way you handle your money as well as how you might become more content and satisfied in your personal as well as your financial lives. In Part II, we will focus on significant life transitions like retirement, marriage, divorce, death and inheritance, for example. These are the types of events that bring people to my door, and they tend to be the times when we can learn most about ourselves in relationship to money. They also tend to be times when our emotions can get the better of us. As we shall see, investigating our relationship to money *before* we undergo these life passages can turn out to be very valuable. In each of the life transitions discussed, I imagine us seated at my conference table discussing your needs, your hopes, your fears, and the ways in which your money can address them. A bit of fair warning: You might be surprised by what you learn about yourself. I'd like to tell you a personal story to illustrate just how blind we sometimes can be to the emotional undercurrents that have been informing our financial decisions without our being aware of them.

A Personal Story

I think people would be surprised, if they thought about it at all, at how quiet the work of a good financial adviser can be. Hollywood has portrayed us as inhabiting a world that's fast-paced and chaotic, filled with young men gesturing wildly, a Bluetooth attached to each ear. In fact, that's not what it's like at all for the majority of advisers who work with investors all around the country. Most of the time our work is very calm. We talk with clients, listen to their stories, and think about how to use investment strategies to solve particular financial problems. We suggest changes in portfolios to take advantage of economic trends, respond to events in the marketplace, or adapt to a change in our client's situation. Surprisingly, a great deal of our work is carried out alone. We work quietly with our clients and their money, and, although there have been some notable Hollywood presentations of greed and trickery in our business, I believe there's no more of that than there is in any other. Most advisers take their responsibilities very seriously.

Of course there are times when working with money is stressful. We deal with so many things that are out of our control: the wide swings in the markets, events all over the globe that affect the financial world, and all the emotions and financial dilemmas that clients bring to our door. All of these factors are interesting, in and of themselves, but to my mind, the most interesting of all is the last of these—our complicated emotional relationships to our money—and it was the one that took me most by surprise.

When I was much younger in my practice, the amount of emotion displayed around money caught me off guard. Nothing in my training had prepared me for it. Somehow I thought decisions would be cut and dried, that they would be based on the numbers and the facts. Early on, I was focused on building my business more than I was on my clients' stories. So imagine my surprise the first time a person began to cry in my office. (He was inheriting money from his mother, who had died suddenly in an accident.) Then there was the couple that got into an argument during our initial meeting because they wanted to do such different things with their money. Or the woman who broke down as she laid out a spreadsheet that showed all the money she had. She was afraid it wasn't enough to last her whole life. There was humor (the artist who had drawn a picture that mapped out where all the family money was) and anger (the young woman who railed against her dead father for leaving her so little) and love (the dying man who gently got his financial house in order before it was too late).

All of these were intriguing to a young adviser. But it was another emotion that surprised me the most of all, the one I saw more than any other. It ran like a current through far too many people's lives and it was rarely helpful: deep, dark fear. This fear seemed to boil over where money was concerned, and it's the one emotion that really got my attention. I was shocked by the amount of fear that I saw. There was the fear of making a mistake and the fear of losing money of course. But even more than these, there was the fear of not having enough, of running out of money. Sometimes this made sense, but often it was completely irrational: There are more than a few millionaires in our midst who are scared to death of outliving their money.

For a long time I observed this phenomenon with interest and detachment. But then one day, as I found myself in one of these life situations where money plays such a large role, I made a startling discovery. I suddenly understood that the reason I saw so much fear around me was not because there was so much fear (although there is quite a bit) but because I shared it. I too had a deep-seated fear of running out of money. I too was convinced that all my best efforts to provide for my family and myself could fall short, and this couldn't have been more irrational! Advising people on how to make their money last was one of the things I did every day. I could see plainly that my personal financial plan was very sound, that I was completely on track. But the numbers and the facts weren't enough to quiet my fears.

Where on earth had this come from? I didn't grow up in a poor family. We certainly weren't wealthy, but we had enough so that we never felt poor. My father was a man who enjoyed thinking about money. He understood it well. He wasn't afraid of a little risk. He liked numbers, and he liked to play with them in his head. But the more I thought about it the more I realized that he was also very afraid of not having enough. His fear, the result of his own upbringing in a family that had to struggle, ran deep. We had a more stable financial life than he had had as a child because he was determined to make it so and because my mother agreed. But the fear had never left him. And amazingly, I had completely absorbed it.

There's a surprising epilogue to this little story of generational fear. My father passed away in 2004, and now it's my mother who handles their money without him. I realize now as I help her sort out the normal financial issues that arise from day to day that she has none of this fear. She's prudent and careful with her money, of course, but she simply doesn't have this deep fear that one day she'll run out. If I think back to my childhood, I can remember many instances when she displayed her "no-fear" approach. My mother had her own career and earned her own money. I was certainly learning money lessons from my mother just as I was from my dad, but in my mind and in my heart, somehow his had prevailed.

So I grew up with two very different models in front of me, one with an element of fear and the other without. But I so thoroughly accepted my father's point of view that I was blind to the fact that my mother's was different. I wonder now how my life would have been different had I adopted her attitude instead of his. I'll never know, of course, but in one sense I'm glad I didn't; had I not had this hidden concern about money, I might not have chosen to become a financial adviser, and I truly believe that my work has been a salvation to me. In many ways, I had to go deep into the world of money to find myself and to relate to others in a fresh new way.

Hidden Attitudes Revealed

I tell this personal story to illustrate the extent to which our emotions go unnoticed when it comes to our money. Our financial attitudes—what we think about money, what we think of others who have more or less than we do, how we choose to spend it or not spend it, what priorities we set as we plan our financial futures—are thoroughly entwined with our deepest emotions. Sometimes we're aware of this fact, and sometimes we're not. And there's no question that we can do foolish things with our money when we're unaware of what drives us. I'm not speaking here so much of what we spend our money on but more of how we use it. I've seen people unconsciously use their money and the power it gives them to punish a family member or to dominate someone else. I've seen people withhold money from family members they love simply to communicate their anger. I've seen wealthy fathers make their children do without basic things for the plain reason that they're afraid to let go of some of their money. I've seen money decisions made out of fear, anger, and greed, all of it barely conscious.

But I've also seen tough decisions made out of love. I've witnessed great acts of generosity and compassion, seen people use their money unceremoniously to help sick friends and care for perfect strangers. It isn't only the negative emotions that drive us; our most admirable virtues can also be expressed through money.

Understanding these financial attitudes and the behaviors that ensue can be invaluable. The point is not only to become better financial decision makers but also to become better people. Observing our relationship to money is an excellent path to greater self-awareness. It opens the door to amazing personal growth.

Many advisers believe that, when it comes to our money decisions, we must set our emotions aside. It's a widely accepted view that strong emotion clouds the rational thinking that financial decisions often require. But I believe it's far subtler than that. I believe that our emotions must inform our decisions. An acknowledgment and real consideration of the emotional framework within which our decisions are being made can only enhance those decisions. From there, rational decisions become far easier.

If fear is what you feel for example, as you make investment decisions, it's worthwhile to investigate it. Fear of what? Why do you feel it? Is it a rational fear or just a sort of knee-jerk reaction? And if it's a reasonable fear, how can it be addressed in the decisions you're making? How can a portion of your portfolio be structured to alleviate this fear? If it's not a rational fear, can you experiment as you make money decisions with a less fearful attitude?

One of the goals of *The Value of Money* is to prompt you to observe yourself in relation to your money, to think about your stories and what they mean, and to uncover the hidden motivations that govern your financial life. With this deeper understanding, you can begin to put your money to work for you on many levels. You can be the master of your financial life. You can learn to see money as the simple tool it is and use it with awareness. You can begin to enjoy money and all the doors it opens. You can leave a legacy with your money that honors you and all that you love. The normal changes that occur as we live our lives provide the triggers that will point us in the right direction.

Money and Our Changing Lives

We tend to think hardest about our money when we're in the middle of one of life's major transitions. Birth, death, retirement, taking over for elderly parents, marriage, divorce, changing jobs—these are times in our lives when our emotions and our money are the most likely to become entangled. At the same time, each of these situations is highly charged emotionally. The truth is that in these types of critical life events, we're called upon to make important financial decisions that can have very long-lasting effects. Fortunately or unfortunately, we're often making our decisions through the haze of emotion that can accompany major change. To expect ourselves to make our decisions with no regard for our strong emotions at these crucial times is simply asking too much. On the other hand, acknowledging and examining our emotions in relation to our money in the midst of change can be very fruitful.

Much of what a good financial adviser does consists of helping clients think through the financial ramifications of change. Financial advisers do spend quite a bit of time staring at a computer screen or studying charts and graphs as one might expect, but the better part of our time—and certainly the most important part—is spent around a conference table listening to clients tell their story. We listen for the details of course—the financial needs, opportunities, and pitfalls—but we also listen for that underlying current of emotion that will be so important to the success of an investment strategy. Sometimes the emotions are buried so deep they're hard to expose. They may, in fact, come as a surprise to the investors themselves. But, at other times, they're just below the surface. They're often the first things we deal with.

I remember a couple that came years ago to consult on their situation. He was thinking of retiring, and they wanted to be assured that they were in good shape. Wisely, they were getting their financial house in order before he made his final decision. When I met them for the first time, I liked them immediately. He was confident, well spoken, and gracious. She was full of life, a graceful woman who had relied on her husband for many years to plan their future. We chatted for a while and then got down to business. He pulled a spreadsheet from his briefcase and laid it out on the table. "Here it is," he said. "This is all we have." As we all leaned in to have a look, I felt a distinct but subtle shift of energy in the room. I looked up at her and was stunned to see tears streaming down her face. Her husband was just as shocked. "I'm so afraid we're going to run out!" she whispered.

How valuable it is to acknowledge and study the ways in which our money and our emotions work together. How important it was for her to express her fear and for her husband and her adviser to recognize it. Consider, for example, another situation: the difficult transition of children taking over the care of elderly parents. In this situation the emotions are undeniable and very important, but so are the money concerns. In the midst of sorrow, confusion, and fear, money considerations loom large. How much is needed? How long will it last? What safety nets are there? What resources? There are few financial situations that we face within families where the responsibility is as great, the beneficiary as helpless, or the emotional landscape as littered with mines! To try to ignore our emotions in such a situation would be almost impossible.

Not all situations are that difficult of course. Sometimes the money issues are quite simple, and it's the emotion that's big. I have, from time to time, advised young expectant parents on the ways in which they can finance a college education for their yet unborn child. Of course, most folks don't start that early, but for the parents who seek me out, discussing the money it might take to fund a college education is often just part of the fun of anticipating a new life with a child.

Sometimes, the money is an unpleasant nuisance in the middle of a big change. It's something that has to be dealt with even though one would rather not. This was certainly the case of the woman whose new employer was terminating her retirement plan on my one extraordinary day. She would have loved to ignore that money, but she was forced to make a decision. As much as she disliked it, she had no choice but to think about money. It's not surprising that it became such a symbol of all her concerns.

Finally, there are situations in which emotion takes the lead. Money becomes nothing but a subcategory of the emotion itself. We see this most often with people who approach everything in their lives with fear. There are times for all of us when investments seem complicated, markets unpredictable, and the future uncertain. For someone who sees everything in life through a lens of fear, money can be especially difficult. There's nothing quite like money and financial decisions in the midst of a life change to bring out the anxiety in a fearful person!

Through all of the transitions that I have witnessed in my clients' lives and in my own, I've seen the full range of emotions and also the financial issues that accompany these changes. I've watched money used as a tool but also as a weapon. I've seen fear, anger, greed, and jealousy, but I've also witnessed inspiring acts of love and compassion, extreme displays of joy and generosity. All of life is here in these transitions, and all of our emotions play out in the ways we handle our money as we go through them. There's no question in my mind that if we wish to understand our emotions better, we can study our money decisions, and if we wish to understand our money situation, we would do well to look at our emotions.

A Great Shift of Wealth

As if our normal day-to-day lives didn't provide us plenty of opportunity to explore this complicated relationship we all have to our money, a major trend in the United States is adding even more fuel to the fire. We are beginning to witness the greatest transfer of wealth our nation has ever seen. Experts estimate that from as little as $41 trillion to as much as $136 trillion will change hands in the coming decades. The sources of this tidal wave of money, which has already begun, are numerous, and we will explore them in Part II. But what is significant in this massive shift of wealth is that it will thrust more and more of us into the role of financial decision makers. This "money in motion" will create an unprecedented opportunity for all of us to explore our emotions around money as well as the ways in which these emotions play out in our financial lives. I dare say, there has never been a better time to undertake this important investigation. The circumstances of our time demand it!

1.

YOU AND YOUR MONEY

It's a rare person indeed who doesn't have a highly charged emotional relationship to money. Whether you're wealthy or poor or somewhere in between, you have probably developed personal attitudes and behaviors around your money that you don't think about too often. And the truth is that these attitudes and behaviors tell the world more about who you really are than you might like.

For example, what comes into your mind (or, better yet, the pit of your stomach) when you think about money? Does it make you feel happy and hopeful? Or does it scare you? Is it fun to think about it or does it bore you to tears? Does the mention of money set you dreaming about what you would do if you had more or scheming about how to get it? Some people find comfort in just counting up what they already have, but others focus only on what they don't have.

No matter what your initial reaction, the truth is that we can learn a great deal about ourselves by looking at what we do when it comes to making decisions about money. Our behavior around it reflects all our basic emotions, from our deepest fears to our fondest wishes. At times, unfortunately, it's where we exercise our worst tendencies, but it can also be where we cultivate our greatest strengths.

Who are you when it comes to your money? Are you the tight-wad or the generous giver? What emotions govern your thinking about it? Fear and anxiety or confidence and joy? What kinds of stories about money did you hear as a child? That you needed to hide it from others? That wealthy people were unhappy and untrustworthy? That money was to be shared?

These are the types of things we will explore in *The Value of Money*. Understanding them is a key to cultivating a rich and peaceful relationship to money, ease in financial decision making, and a special type of self-awareness.

Fear, Love, and Money

Money is many things to many people. It can be a weapon, an object of desire, a tool for generous compassion, or a symbol of success. Seen in this light, it really is a stage on which we play out all of our dramas. In my many years of working with people and their money, I've seen over and over the ways in which we bring our emotions into our financial lives, and I've also seen how our finances can rule over our emotional lives. All of this can be good, of course, but it can also be very bad. Most of the time, we're blind to the complicated relationship between money and emotion, and sometimes that lack of awareness can have terrible consequences. One client's story illustrates just how complicated things can get.

Sylvia was a lovely woman with a very good job in a large corporation. As an executive with this company, she had been given an opportunity to retire in her midfifties and was offered a very attractive retirement package. Sylvia was friendly and relaxed, clearly a woman accustomed to making decisions. She announced her retirement to me with great certainty about her future. She didn't display any of the anxiety that many feel as they move into this stage of life. We talked casually and pleasantly about the transition she was making before getting down to the business of examining her financial situation. Finally, we settled into discussing her portfolio in light of this change in her life.

I recognized immediately a fairly common problem. Like a lot of executives, Sylvia had most of her money in company stock, but, unlike many executives, she was especially "married" to it: She loved it. She was faithful to it. She trusted it. In large measure, she had created her wealth through this company. Of course, she was tied to it. It was a very good stock but an aggressive one, and, because her money was concentrated in that one stock, it made the entire portfolio quite aggressive. Now, however, she was entering into the retirement phase of her financial life, a time when many investors wish to become more conservative. When I suggested that we would need to sell some of this stock in order to balance her portfolio, she seemed somewhat shocked. That was out of the question; it would constitute a betrayal. She had given her working life to this company, and it had always been good to her. Selling this stock would have been like an odd form of adultery. Her faith in her company was so complete that she couldn't imagine a scenario where heavy concentration in that one stock would be dangerous, where having all her eggs in that particular basket wouldn't pay off.

If the stock had been a conservative one, I might have felt a bit more comfortable, but it was not. It was an aggressive one in a highly competitive and changeable industry and despite my recommendation that my client sell at least a portion of her stock, she opted to keep it all. The challenge now became working around it with what little other money was available to offer her greater diversification.

For a while, it seemed to go well enough. But, after a year or two, her company began to go through a rough period. The competition in its industry was fierce. One of its key leaders left the firm and took a number of other important people with him. The company began to temporarily lose its way. Then, on top of all that, the stock market itself went into a major correction, a downturn that took all stock values down. There was absolutely nothing out there to make this stock go up or to keep it from going down. It fell through the floor, dropping in value by more than 50 percent, as did, of course, the largest part of her portfolio. Sylvia was horrified, dismayed, and angry with herself. But more than that, she was angry with her company; the company to whom she had given so much had betrayed her. It wasn't the end of the world. She still had enough money left, but her future was less secure than it could have been. Blind emotion had ruled the day, and it had cost her dearly.

What I hope for you is that you can learn to know yourself better *before* you come to the crossroads of an important financial decision like the one Sylvia had to make. As you read on, I hope to help you uncover who you really are with regard to money. "But, who I am has nothing to do with money," you might say. Well, hear me out and perhaps you will be surprised just how much who you are relates to what you do with your money and what you do with your money relates to who you are.

The Flow of Money in Our Lives

Money is a current that runs through every aspect of our lives. It influences the work we do, the health-care choices we make, the towns we live in, the way we raise our children. It becomes part of our decisions regarding marriage, birth, and death. In one way or another, it's a part of all of life's milestones, even if only a very small one. In so many of the ordinary and even the extraordinary things that we do, we must deal with money. Even those who claim not to care about it must focus on it to some extent. It's just part of life, the simple tool we use to provide for ourselves and our families and our communities. But like so many other things in our lives, sometimes we make it very complicated.

I've never taken one of those vacations where all expenses are paid ahead of time, but I know that one of the intriguing parts of these kinds of trips has to do with money. Once the trip begins, the vacationer has no need of it. No need to pay for food or drinks; they've already been paid for. No need to buy a ticket for a show since it's all been paid for. Friends who have taken these trips say it's amazingly relaxing to not handle money at all. They love that you never have to ask yourself, "Can I afford this today?" "Is this extra show in my budget?" It's really an opportunity to pretend that money is no object, that everything we see we can have. People say that not handling money offers an unexpected feeling of freedom. These trips are not only a vacation from routine life but evidently also a vacation from money. The very fact that people enjoy these breaks demonstrates to me that, for some at least, money exerts a little pressure all the time and that it exerts a lot of pressure some of the time.

But money isn't complicated only because, at times, we don't have enough or because sometimes we want to do things we can't afford. It isn't difficult only because the choices we have to make about our money have long-term ramifications for others as well as ourselves. And even the many calculations that sometimes accompany money aren't, to my mind, the greatest source of difficulty. Our complicated relationship to money goes much deeper than that. Money is complicated because we make it complicated. We tangle it up with all of our fears, our strengths, and our weaknesses. Over and over I've seen people use their money as a weapon to hurt others or to dominate them. I've seen folks use their money to express disdain or disapproval. I've seen them use it to inflate their own egos. But just as often I have seen them put their money to the service of love, compassion, and joy. Luckily, we don't use money only to express our worst tendencies. We can also use it to exercise our greatest virtues. But first we need to know who we are in relationship to it.

We All Have a Style

Over the years, I've advised countless individuals, families, and organizations on their finances. I've seen financial decisions made in a variety ways. I've worked with many people who are excellent decision makers. These are calm, reflective, and organized folks who listen well and understand their own needs.

But I've also dealt with many people for whom the decisions are a struggle. There are those, for example, who bury themselves in a study of the details. Of course, this may be a healthy and mature way to get a handle on the subject matter in order to make an informed decision, but for many this endless research is a way of postponing a decision. They immerse themselves in the details, hoping against hope that they will achieve some sort of clarity or that somehow decisions will be made for them. This type of stalling is certainly not the worst thing a person can do, but it can make the whole process so complicated that it's a wonder any decision ever gets made!

Other decision makers abdicate all responsibility. They want, more than anything, to simply turn it all over to someone else. They strongly resist an active role for themselves. This approach is acceptable to a point, and in certain circumstances it can be very appropriate. But good financial advisers always want your input. They can guide you toward appropriate decisions, make recommendations, and advise you on all the different areas of financial life, but they should always do so with a tremendous amount of information and feedback from you, the person who, as we say, "owns" the money. As much as financial advisers care—and good ones care a great deal more than they're given credit for—they will never be as close to your money as you are.

And then there are the decision makers who just want to get it over with. I suppose that many of these folks just aren't too interested in the subject of money (and there's nothing that says everyone should be interested). A quick decision isn't necessarily a bad one. But, in my opinion, simply "getting it over with" misses a valuable opportunity to consider a whole other dimension that *The Value of Money* is meant to demonstrate. Every financial decision is an opportunity to explore not only the financial world but also your own complicated emotional landscape. Every decision presents an opportunity to step back, examine yourself, and then choose what's most appropriate for you. And every decision is also a chance to grow, especially if a little self-examination reveals an unfulfilling pattern of behavior.

So what type of decision maker might you be? It isn't hard to begin to understand. Think about the last time you had a financial decision to make, especially one that felt large to you. Do you remember how you felt about the responsibility? Was your basic attitude toward the whole thing one of fear or one of excitement? Realizing what your basic attitude was in that situation makes it easier to understand your behavior. Did you dive into your decision making with gusto, or did you put things off as long as you could?

What does making financial decisions mean to you? Some find it gives them a great sense of independence and maturity; others feel resentful and overwhelmed. And if there were other people involved in your decision, how did you feel about them? Competitive, cooperative? Did they help or hinder? These are the type of issues *The Value of Money* encourages you to explore as we talk about the normal life events that so often bring our money and our emotions not only into sharp focus but also deep conflict.

The Seven Basic Types of Money Relationships

I've always been interested in money. It's a fascinating topic in and of itself. As our world becomes smaller and our economy increasingly global, those of us who pay attention to money can be plugged into an entire universe of news and influences and investment possibilities. Major events all over the globe are quickly reflected in our stock and bond markets. Opportunities for investments in other parts of the world become more common and more important every day. I will never cease to be fascinated by the ways in which money makes money as it circulates around the world.

As interesting as money can be, however, it isn't the most compelling part of the work I've done all these years. To me, nothing is more intriguing than that complex dynamic that arises when people interact with their money. By themselves, people and money are interesting. Together, they form a rich tapestry of stories, emotions, inspiration, and admonitions.

Everyone is different, of course, but over the years, I've observed seven basic types of relationships to money. Each has many variations, many different manifestations, and I suspect that most of us display traits of all of these styles at various times in our lives or with different pools of money. Nonetheless, it's useful I believe to describe these basic types as touchstones for our exploration. Throughout *The Value of Money,* we will see them all demonstrated.

The "Money-Is-King" Type

For people who approach their finances in this way, money is an end in and of itself. It's the measure by which all things are judged, including their own lives. Although they might never care to admit it, for these individuals, money trumps everything else. This attitude may lead them to shortchange other things in their lives in favor of money, important things like relationships or even their own happiness. They measure all things—themselves, others, their work, their relationships, etcetera—using money as the yardstick.

There can be many manifestations of this type of relationship to money, but it isn't hard to recognize. And let me hasten to add that it isn't always a bad thing. But if you ever find yourself automatically judging a wealthy person more favorably than one less wealthy, for example, you might lean in this direction. Or if you have ever sacrificed your own personal satisfaction for the sake of some extra money alone or if all of your dreams for the future relate to how much you can earn, you may give money the sort of dominance in your life that this type of relationship fosters.

The "Little-Lamb" Type

People who remain like children in relation to their money refuse to ever assume responsibility themselves. Their childlike attitude leads them to act in all sorts of irresponsible ways, from spending recklessly to giving total control over their financial future to another. On some level, money and all that goes with it are threats, and never assuming responsibility, the best defense. Most of these people fear money, I suspect. They fear the mistakes one can make or the responsibility of making decisions or simply facing the realities that money imposes on us all. Remaining a child in relation to their money allows them to never face their money straight on and therefore never face the tough issues.

This is the "I'll think about it tomorrow!" approach to money management. We most often see it displayed by individuals who proclaim that they "could never possibly understand all that money stuff" and so they simply don't ever try.

The "I'll-Pick-Up-the-Bill-If-You-Just..." Type

In the hands of manipulative people, money is an incredible weapon, the means by which they dominate, punish, and express disapproval. An angry person can wage war with others by using money in all sorts of ways that seem surprisingly acceptable or even respectable. Amazingly, angry individuals can use money to express and hide their anger at the same time. They can appear to be acting in another's best interest even as they're expressing disdain and disapproval. Money is a particularly effective tool with which manipulative and/or angry people can act out their anger.

Have you even been gleeful at another person's financial misfortune? Do you try to keep other family members or coworkers ignorant of financial details that would be useful to them? These kinds of behaviors often belie a willingness to use money as a weapon. They're symptoms of an angry relationship.

The "Wolf-Never-Leaves-My-Door" Type

Some people will always fear the wolf at the door, no matter how much money they amass. For them, the poverty that they fear will always be more real than the wealth they may acquire, but acquiring it will always be important since it's the vital link to safety. For individuals who fear for their own security, whether they do it consciously or not, money is a constant focus. There can never be enough because there will always be danger.

This type of relationship is easy to recognize. Many of us have a little bit of it within us to contend with. It's marked by fear; fear of running out of money, fear of losing it, fear of someone else taking it or having more than their share of it. If you have ever felt a little poor and then received some money to put away for a rainy day and then immediately felt poor again, you may experience this type of connection to your money. But happily, these fears are not difficult to work with. They are quite common, but they can be overcome.

The "Money Martyr"

For people who see themselves as victims, money is an especially effective tool. They can undermine themselves with rash decisions or unrealistic expectations or they can allow themselves to be undermined by others in a wide variety of ways. Money provides us with many opportunities for self-sabotage. For a person bent on being a victim, money, like so many other things in life, can easily provide the means.

Have you ever chosen a financial path that people you trusted had told you was doomed to failure? Have you ever lost money in an investment because you stubbornly insisted you knew what you were doing when, in fact, you hadn't really done your homework? Have you ever spent wildly with no regard to how much money you actually had? If so, you might be a money martyr.

The "All-Is-Well" Type

At this point it may seem to you that I've only witnessed troubled relationships to money, but in fact I have had the privilege of observing many people who display a very peaceful connection to their money. There are many who approach money with decisiveness and confidence. They appreciate money for what it is: a simple tool. They remain at ease and graceful with it. They may be wealthy or not by society's standards, but it hardly matters; they are at peace. Money is a part of that peace, but it's not the cause. It's simply a part of their total picture of health and well being.

If what you feel is confidence and calm about money issues— whether you're wealthy or not—you've undoubtedly developed a peaceful relationship to your money. For you, all will be well, no matter what happens.

The "Spread-the-Joy" Type

And finally, there are those who understand that great joy is to be had in using money with generosity and compassion. These lucky folks are never controlled by their money. They use it in ways that express their deepest values and their best selves. Not only are they at peace with their money in their lives, but they also use it with awareness for their own good and for the good of others.

Do you often think about your money and the ways in which it relates to your dreams or the dreams of those you love? Have you ever ignored what others were telling you you should own or do with your money in order to put it toward some good that you care deeply about? If so, you understand this "Spread-the-Joy" type of money relationship. And you are a fortunate person indeed!

You may or may not recognize yourself in one or more of these descriptions, but I hope that as we move into Part II to address the life situations that so many of us will be facing in the coming years, you will understand yourself a bit better. I hope that you will recognize not only the weaknesses in your relationship to money but also the strengths. Together, I hope that we can begin to cultivate the relationship you seek, that we can all move toward the peaceful and joyful relationships that make money such a worthwhile and useful part of our lives.

The Potential of This Journey

As I will say over and over in this book, money is a plain and simple tool. But oh what importance we give it! We allow it to play a variety of roles in our lives, most of them quite positive. Beyond the necessities of food and shelter, money permits us to do things that we want or need to do: get an education, take care of our families and friends, buy nice clothes, or just play golf. It provides security for our old age and backing for the projects we take on.

Many people do go further in their thinking about money than just enjoying what they can do or buy with it. For many of us, money is a major indicator of success in our lives, a reward for hard work or an incentive to do more. It's a source of pride or shame. We all—or most of us—keep our eyes on our money to make sure there's enough to support our lifestyles or build toward the lifestyle we would like. Some of us have a deep need to strive for more in order to achieve a goal or prove something to ourselves, but we rarely go further.

We spend time counting money and thinking about it, gathering it up, and, of course, spending it. But we rarely give thought to a dimension of money that I have come to believe is the hidden treasure in our financial lives, one that is deep, provocative, and exciting.

The truth is that money, like relationships or health or work, is a looking glass through which we can glimpse our inner life. Every financial decision shines a light on the way in which our emotions dictate our behavior. Our biggest financial decisions, and even our smallest at times, can lay bare those emotions that form the cornerstones of our experiences. Whatever emotions we feel when we have to make a financial decision are probably emotions that permeate our lives. Understanding how our money and our emotions work together makes the financial decisions easier, of course, but it also can lead to spiritual growth and greater self-awareness.

I believe that with greater self-awareness will come the desire to work with money in new and better ways. We have an opportunity that we ought not to miss, a chance to wake up about our money and to raise the level of awareness of the positive potential of this incredible tool in our lives and in our communities. We have the opportunity to change our very consciousness about money.

2.

- -

SPIRITUAL POTENTIAL

Over the years I've come to believe that we are all here on earth to create experiences for ourselves from which to learn some specific lessons, lessons that we choose. Throughout our lives, the circumstances of day-to-day existence combine in ways that provide us opportunities to learn what we need or wish to learn. No matter what we may think we're doing as we go about our normal routines, work toward our goals, raise our families, and so on, beneath it all there is always something to learn. Witness the ways in which so many of us repeat our mistakes until we finally understand the lesson those mistakes have to teach us. We're constantly pursuing, in one form or another, the experiences that help us to fulfill our mission on this earth. It may not even be important that we know what lessons we seek. We have only to live our lives with awareness. If compassion—for ourselves, others, and the world at large—guides us, we will surely succeed.

The specific circumstances of our lives may not even be important factors. Lessons are available in all circumstances, no matter how big or how small. For example, our life goal may not be about learning to speak French, but doing so may open our world in ways that show us how we limit ourselves with our narrow-mindedness, and that might be the lesson we need to learn. Achieving a life goal of flying a plane or climbing a mountain may not be why we've come into this life, but learning to focus our energies or appreciate the power and majesty of nature might be. It's often a simple matter of looking beyond the circumstance itself to see what larger issue it reveals.

I even believe that we can think differently about some life goals that are larger or nobler than learning a language or flying a plane. Surely to raise a happy, healthy, and successful family would be enough for a life well lived. Beyond that obvious success and reward, however, there lie lessons of deep responsibility, self-sacrifice, and care. Likewise, running a successful enterprise— a corporation or an organization of any kind—has enormous rewards in terms of money and ego. Yet, viewed in terms of our soul's contract, that too could be about far more. Such success could really be about providing for others, exercising creativity, or acting on a vision. As important as the circumstances of our lives may be in and of themselves, their greater and deeper value may be hidden and quite unexpected.

Of course we all want to know why we're here. And it's tempting to look at another's situation and judge what someone else should be learning! (Obviously, this is a terrible trap and needs to be avoided at all costs. Our own lives offer us enough to deal with!) But, in fact, it may not be that important that we understand or decide exactly what our life is about. Perhaps it's only important that we go about all that we do with awareness and compassion, watching for opportunities to grow, learn, and expand. Perhaps the most important thing is to step back from all of our dramas, conflicts, excitements, successes, and failures, and just observe. From there it's an easy step to embracing our lessons.

Money, like so many other things in our lives, provides these windows into our spiritual lives. In fact, it provides more of them than most things. Big, small, good, bad—money is everywhere in our lives. Every day we deal with it in one way or another. Money can be one of our greatest teachers, and as such, it is quite special. Because it's so much a part of all the aspects of our lives, it offers us a wide variety of lessons, different lessons in different circumstances and at different stages of our lives. Some of these lessons can be quite vivid and profound; others quiet and very subtle. And, because we deal with it so much, money offers us learning opportunities over and over, giving us many chances to get it right.

A Great Tool

Many people in our society believe that money tempts us to evil, but through my work with people and their money, I have often witnessed that it tempts us to good every bit as much. In truth, it's neither of these, of course. In and of itself, money is absolutely neutral. It's a tool in our lives and an especially powerful one at that. If money tempts us to arrogance or greed or cruelty, it's because we allow it to. If it tempts us to generosity and compassion, it's because that's what we seek. Money can only be what we make of it in our lives, and therein lies its great potential. We can make it a tool for whatever we deem to be the most important thing. We can use it just as consciously for good as we can for ill.

. . .

But how do we begin to understand the meaning of money in our lives, let alone the ways in which it reflects our deeper truths or points the way to spiritual growth? The answer is observation of ourselves, first and foremost, of our past experiences, and of what in them might be shaping our present decisions.

Years ago, I was inspired by a client and friend who demonstrated to me some of money's healing potential. She was and remains a person of extraordinary strength who wasn't afraid to know the truth about herself. I first met Marie as she was coming to the end of a rather long and drawn-out divorce. As the whole ugly process was coming to a close, she was tired and a bit depressed but definitely ready to get on with her life. When we first sat down together, Marie had already worked through a number of the emotional stages that accompany separation and divorce. She was ready to move on to the next stage of her life, which made her decisions a bit more straightforward when it came to her money. She was very easy to work with and plan for, and a fun person besides. We got busy designing and implementing a strategy for the rather sizable amount of money she received in her divorce settlement.

Things went along fine for a while until I began to notice the amount of money that was being spent. Marie had definitely begun spending more than we were making in her investments. She was eating away at her money pretty quickly. Since she was only in her early fifties, I began to be alarmed that this money, even though there was a lot of it, wasn't going to last her. And so, Marie and I began to have a series of rather uneasy discussions about her budget.

These types of conversations are always uncomfortable ones for financial advisers. No one likes to be told they're spending too much money and need to cut back, and, frankly, no one likes to deliver that news. If Marie had been elderly, I wouldn't have worried. Using up some of the money wouldn't have been a problem. But at the age that she was and at the pace she was spending, time was not on her side. I did some rough calculations for her and estimated that, at the rate she was going, she would run out of money in about fifteen years.

Marie agreed to meet me for coffee, and I prepared mentally for a conversation that I knew would be unhappy. Honestly, I was very concerned that she wouldn't be able or somehow wouldn't be willing to curtail her spending. I was worried that, despite all my best efforts, she really would run out of money. As much as I hated to lay this all out in front of her, I felt a deep responsibility to do just that. The truth was, I was scared for her.

We met at a local coffee shop and chatted for some time catching up. All the while, of course, my mind was rehearsing what I wanted to say. Finally, I began spelling out the situation as plainly as I could: We can earn money in the investments, but not quickly enough to support your current level of spending. You've begun to dip down into the principal or core of your investment portfolio. You will run out of money by age sixty-five.

I'll never forget the look on her face. Fear, disbelief, anger but then, very quickly, businesslike concern. Marie asked me a number of questions and then promised to go home and go over her budget thoroughly. I felt relieved of course, but I was still scared for her.

The next day Marie called me and asked me to meet her once again. She wanted, she said, to tell me a story. This time, I was the one who listened. I couldn't have been more surprised or, frankly, more inspired.

Marie filled me in on a part of her past that she hadn't spoken of before. She told me how for many years, she had had a terrible problem with alcohol. Year after year, she lived what appeared to be a very successful life but one that was, in fact, controlled by secret drinking. Then one day, quite by accident, she found herself at a gathering where alcoholism was the topic. Although she had heard people talk about the path to recovery before, she had never had much interest. That day, for some reason, the speaker's words went straight to her heart. She went home, called a treatment center, and began the long journey to health.

Now, some fifteen years later, she felt privileged to live her life every day. She told me with tears in her eyes that her mother had died at a fairly young age. Had Marie not stopped drinking, she felt certain that she would have as well. But now, because alcohol no longer controlled her, she "got to live the life my mother never had."

As I listened to her though, I wondered how this story was related to her money. Marie told me that she had gone home after our conversation the day before and spent the evening doing some genuine soul searching. She realized, she said, that excessive spending was the exact same pattern of behavior as excessive drinking. As much as she hated to admit it, she knew that she had to tackle this challenge just as she had tackled the earlier one. And fortunately for her, because of her past, she knew how.

Years before, she had confronted her own alcoholism and slowly gotten control of her life. Then divorce hit her, and she had to learn how to stand on her own two feet as a single woman. And now money was offering her yet another opportunity to take control and be independent. She would get control of her budget.

Over the next several months, I watched Marie's spending change. She cut back on her expenses as promised. She became aware of her money and what she did with it in a way she never had before. She absolutely took charge of this part of her life in order to live within her means and enjoy the fruits of her new responsibility and independence. Not only did we see her portfolio stop shrinking, but we also began to see her money grow!

It would be easy to say that Marie really didn't have much of a choice here, but that's not true at all. There were certainly other ways that she could have responded to this challenge. She could have felt sorry for herself and many people would have. She could have stuck her head in the sand and ignored my warnings. She could have gone out to find another person to "take care" of her and continued to spend away. But Marie rose to the challenge. She saw budgeting as part of her pattern of growing health and independence. She saw her personal budget crisis as just the opportunity she needed to go where her spirit wanted. As her financial adviser, I breathed a sigh of relief. As her friend, I watched with admiration and awe.

Blinded by Fear

But not everyone is as determined to grow as Marie. Not everyone is able to think through the dynamics of their relationship to money. Not everyone wants to. These dynamics are complicated, and sometimes they challenge us in ways that we'd rather not acknowledge. Or for some the money habits are so deeply ingrained as to be all but invisible.

Another client with whom I worked many years ago was an

elderly man of considerable wealth. Although my relationship with him was quite cordial, I couldn't help notice how much he focused on the negative side of things. He often complained at length about things that were completely out of his control. Still, despite this negative side, I enjoyed working with him well enough. One day, he began to tell me about his daughter. She was going through a rough period in her life. Divorced, with two young children, she was searching for a job and having trouble finding one. She desperately needed money for herself and for her kids, and everything pointed to this being a temporary situation for them. Inheriting her father's money one day was fine, but it didn't help her right then, when she really needed help.

My client described to me how he had bought some clothes and school supplies for his grandkids and was even planning on paying some of his daughter's bills for a few months until things improved, but it bothered him to do this, not because he didn't want to help, but because he saw it as an added expense for him. He fretted and complained terribly. His fear of this extra expense made him stingy with her. The sum he was giving to his daughter was only enough money, it seemed to me, to take the edge off the family's suffering: it was certainly enough to help her, but not enough to relieve the stress she was under.

I well remember the phone conversation we had about this situation. He complained about the terrible economy: His daughter couldn't find an adequate job. He spoke of his grandchildren's father who couldn't seem to take care of his family. He bemoaned how hard all this was for his daughter, how she was struggling. Amazingly, he worried aloud about what the extra expense of helping her and her family would mean to his budget. I had a very disjointed feeling as I listened to him. With my ears I heard his words, but with my eyes, I looked at my computer screen: There were literally millions of dollars in his account with us. It seemed incredible to me, almost impossible. How was it that this man could honestly fear that what he was giving his daughter would put his own security at risk? How could he not see that the millions of dollars he had would be more than enough to sustain him for his lifetime, enough so that he could easily share some of it with her? Could not at least some of this money find its way to his daughter, a person whom he clearly loved very much? How could he focus so much on her difficult situation and not see that he was in a position to relieve at least a bit of its harshness?

I knew as we spoke that, even though he was helping his daughter to make ends meet, his help was not enough to keep her from feeling poor. "Poverty" was deeply ingrained in this family. Despite his considerable wealth, feeling poor was what my client really understood. His tremendous fear of not having enough money was the very thing that perpetuated his daughter's hardship. The hardship that she experienced and that he watched her experience was the very one that he feared most for himself. Her situation somehow reinforced the feeling of poverty that so pervaded his own being. Despite the fact that he bemoaned her situation, somehow, for him, it was the way things were. For his daughter's part, feeling poor and stressed would no doubt instill her father's fear deep in her own heart, keeping it alive for yet another generation.

The dynamic set in motion by his fear of shortage was a very complicated one. Rather than empowering her, he kept her tied to his charity. Rather than allowing her situation to be the source of change, to become an opportunity for him to confront his fear and let it go, he chose to perpetuate this cycle. Her difficult situation gave him something to moan about. It fueled a general pessimism

47

he had about the world at large, society, young people, and so on. It confirmed all his fears and reinforced them, making him even more adamant about holding on to his money. But most of all, it frightened him; poverty was what he feared most. No matter what his account value was, poverty was what he believed in. It was his fear, not his net worth, that created "poverty" for him. As I looked at his account, I could see millions of dollars. He could look at the same and see only a war chest.

Both of these clients faced challenging situations stemming from their deep and complicated relationship to money. Money offered both an opportunity to step back and do the kind of self-examination that's so difficult for us all but almost always leads to growth. One embraced the challenge; the other couldn't recognize it.

In my opinion, this is the great potential of money in our lives and one that we almost always overlook. The lessons are there for the taking, and they're filled with personal, emotional, and spiritual rewards. Unfortunately, though, the path isn't always easy. Sometimes, most times in fact, this sort of self-examination requires real courage and a kind of pure honesty that many of us are inclined to avoid.

Key Spiritual Lessons

Most situations in our lives beg the deeper issues. Most situations point the way to some important lesson if we care to look on them in that way. Our money situations are no exception.

Observing ourselves closely is the key to sorting out the spiritual potential of our financial lives. Once we begin, our world expands, our financial lives become a bit simpler, and our insights begin to spill over into other parts of our lives.

For years I have observed both myself and others in relation to money with an eye to understanding the key spiritual lessons available in that complicated world of finance. Although there are surely more and many variations on spiritual themes in the money world, these five are the principal lessons I've observed. It's my hope that you will recognize these lessons throughout *The Value of Money* as they are manifested in its many stories and that you will begin to explore them in your own financial life.

What we give to the world is given to us.

This is an old adage, of course, but "What goes around, comes around" plays out in especially vivid ways in the world of money.

"What goes around, comes around" may sound a bit vague, but, in fact, where money is concerned, things tend to become very concrete. Let me offer a story that illustrates the first of our lessons in a particularly tangible and even humorous way.

Many clients routinely make gifts from their investment portfolio to their favorite charities. A financial adviser's job is to help an individual determine which stock or bond would be the best to give and then to facilitate the transfer—a very simple task overall. But I often find it interesting to watch these transfers take place.

Years ago, a wealthy client decided to offer his church a particular stock out of his portfolio. Within six months, he was surprised to receive a gift himself from a rather distant relative. To his amazement, his gift was the exact same stock he had given away and almost exactly the same amount. "Well shoot!" he laughed. "If I'd known I was going to get it all back, I would have given all my money away!" His gift, offered with an open and generous heart, came back to him in the most concrete way imaginable.

Now, of course, there's no guarantee that if you give some of your money away, it will be returned to you. But it is clear that generosity begets generosity. A gracious and generous attitude toward money encourages an equally gracious and generous experience. What we give the world, the world gives back to us. Logically, then, it must follow that what we withhold from the world will be withheld from us. This cause-and-effect dynamic is also at work in the world of money. Those who think themselves "poor" will be poor, no matter how much money is in their coffers. Those who are generous will receive as well.

There are only two emotions: love and fear.

Love and fear, in all their many manifestations, show themselves in countless ways in the world of money, just as they do in other aspects of our lives. When we are making financial decisions, love—joy, compassion, generosity—is a very positive, constructive force. Fear, on the other hand—anger, greed, jealousy—is a horribly destructive one. At the end of the day, all of the emotions that money illicits come down to some form of these two.

The story of my client who had such difficulty helping his daughter is an example of this dichotomy. Ultimately, the relationship that he had with her, and especially with her over money, came down to these two emotions. Of course he loved his daughter, and he did express his love by helping her and her children out financially, but in his heart, his great fear of running out of money did battle with his love for his family.

All of his negativity spoke of his fear: his tremendous fear of shortage, his deep need to protect himself in the world. And I judge him not for this fear. No doubt it was the result of very negative past experiences. But here was a clear example of the way in which love and fear can play out in our financial lives. In the conflict he felt over this issue of helping his daughter by giving her some of his money, all was stripped down to these two basic emotions. He loved her as much as any father would, but his fear was so great that it tempered all of his actions.

Money is the mirror in which we glimpse our true selves.

Our money decisions put our hidden motivations on display whether we realize it or not. If we seek to understand ourselves better—and improve ourselves by becoming more compassionate and generous people—we have only to observe ourselves in relation to our money.

For years I've worked with folks as they retire and make the financial decisions that will determine how their money will flow for the rest of their lives. I've witnessed the nervousness, uncertainty, and discomfort people feel in the face of these important decisions. I thought I understood these concerns until recently, when I myself had to make a number of irrevocable decisions on my own pension. To my great surprise, it scared me a little! I worked and reworked the numbers. Finally I made my choices but not without realizing how sobering they were. These decisions— when would I like to retire, how do I want to live once I do, what do I want to do with my money once I'm in retirement, how much will I need, and so on—will affect the rest of my life. It's not that I haven't thought about these things before; I have and quite often. But I never had had to think them through and then make the concrete financial decisions to make them happen. I never had had to commit to these priorities in such a material and tangible way before. The financial side of a routine life event—the kind of event that so many of us will face over the coming years—forced my hand and threw me temporarily into that complicated tangle of money and emotion that I have been observing for so many years.

Having to make a few significant financial decisions pushed me to sort out a number of my own values and to consider the relationship between those values and my money. I thought I understood all these issues from years of helping others work through them, but helping someone else was nothing like doing it for myself. I really had no idea what that process actually feels like or how it can take you into yourself if you're willing to allow it. Money can be the mirror we use for this sort of investigation, and, because it's so linked to the practical aspects of our lives, it's an especially truthful mirror at that.

Money is the bridge between our values and our material world.

No matter what we say we value most, how we handle our money will reveal our true priorities. Beyond that though, money can be the instrument we use to cultivate the most important values we wish to exemplify. Money can be a form of self-expression, and, with awareness, it can express our most cherished values.

The story of my own nervousness over an important set of

decisions points to a greater potential that money offers. Dealing with my choices forced me to sort out some priorities for the rest of my life, but then the question became how to use that money to express those values, how to put my money into the service of my goals. As I made my choices, I came full circle from money being the mirror to my inner self to money being the bridge to my material life. It went something like this: Knowing that my money decisions will affect my future life, I will seriously explore what's really important to me, and then, once I know what's really important, I set up my money in ways that will support my priorities. It sounds logical and practical, but in fact many of us don't take the opportunity that money decisions offer. We don't really think concretely about what we want or what we value, and we don't consciously put our money into the service of those desires. Too often we just roll along and make the simpler decisions or the decisions that another recommends, or we try to keep things the way they've always been. We resist the hard work of exploring ourselves and then figuring out ways to allow our money to express what we believe in. But this process of exploration is full of potential, and the money decisions we're all called upon to make in our lives invite us to this very creative form of self-expression.

Money has no intrinsic power.

We certainly do afford money great power in our society! We give it power in our lives, our families, our communities, and our world that it simply doesn't have on its own. We are the ones who decide what power money should have. So, of course, it stands to reason that we can give money any power we choose and as much of it as we wish. We can give it spiritual power just as easily as any other.

People who have money seem more powerful, but it isn't the money that gives them the power; it's how they use it, how they feel about themselves in relation to it. There have been many powerful people in the world who have not been wealthy by any financial measure. Likewise, there are those who have a great deal of money but don't wield any special power in our world. And there are societies in which things other than money bestow power on individuals.

Money is only a societal invention, an efficient tool developed so that we can easily exchange goods and services. As anyone who has it knows, it doesn't buy happiness, although it can open doors to many possibilities. As I have seen over and over, a wealthy person can be as miserable as a poor one. Likewise, all of us can be happy, no matter what our financial status is. Money has no intrinsic power, but it can be put to very powerful use. And that's the goal of this book: that we all realize the potential our money gives us and begin to use it consciously and in meaningful ways.

Money—A Tool for Growth

The lessons that we can derive from examining our emotional relationship to money offer us not only the hope of becoming better financial decision makers but also better people. As with my friend Marie, these lessons can lead us toward a better life. They can make us more generous, more compassionate, and, ultimately, more free. They're lessons that improve our relationship to ourselves and to others by offering the hope of less fear and more joy. Our money can be a tool for spiritual growth, not only in what we spend it on but also in our relationship to it. If we're brave enough to permit it, money can be the gateway to profound personal growth.

Although this spiritual potential has been the most surprising discovery I've made while working in this world of money, it seems obvious to me now. Of course we can know ourselves more thoroughly by examining our relationship to our money. Of course we can express our values through our money just as surely as we can through so many other aspects of our lives. Our handling of our money reveals us just as surely as does our child rearing or the way we conduct our businesses, run our homes, or take care of our health.

The legacy we leave through our money is as much a spiritual one as it is a material one. As so much money changes hands in the next decades, we have the opportunity to enter a brave new money world filled with challenge and opportunity. My fondest hope is that we will all approach this transition consciously. Now is the time to decide exactly what we want our money to say about us. Now is the time to begin to use our money as a tool to probe the deepest levels of our emotional and our spiritual lives.

II.

Your Changing Life and Your Money

The greatest transfer of wealth in the history of the United States has already begun. According to John J. Havens and Paul G. Schervish of the Boston College Social Welfare Research Institute, this movement of money began in roughly 1998 and will extend to approximately 2052. They believe we will see anywhere from $41 trillion to $136 trillion change hands during this period. In the financial world, we call this "money in motion," and our nation has never seen more of it at one time. And if there is one thing I've learned in these almost twenty-five years in the financial world, it's that money in motion causes anxiety.

This great shift of wealth—a veritable tidal wave of dollars—has been set in motion by a number of forces. First, there is our aging population, led by a now-elderly generation of savers. As the oldest Americans gradually pass away, large amounts of money will be spread throughout society. Their wealth will pass to their family members, of course, but it will also be transferred to churches, educational organizations, charitable foundations, and to the government in the form of taxes.

Inheritance, however, isn't the only source of this great movement of money. There's also the second force behind this shift of wealth: the retirement of the baby boomers. I am a part of this segment of the population about which so much has been made. We, the baby boomers, have been characterized less by our ability to save and more by our desire to examine, transform, question, and revolutionize every aspect of American life. By our sheer numbers, we've created markets and changed industries as we pass through the normal stages of life. Now we're entering this new period of life, a new phase to be explored: retirement.

The baby boomers are beginning to make decisions on what is for many people the largest single pool of money they will ever work with—the money they held in employer-sponsored retirement plans. Many retirees choose to transfer portions of this money into Individual Retirement Accounts where they can control it themselves. Others choose to handle things differently. Either way, what to do with a 401(k) or a 403(b) is a big decision and should be thoroughly discussed with a qualified adviser.

But that's just the beginning. With retirement come money decisions that affect the rest of our lives. As the baby boomers decide how to invest retirement money and how to live off of it once they're no longer working, they're beginning to face tough money issues and a whole host of other difficult decisions. For those contemplating retirement, "Will I have enough?" is a primary concern. This is followed closely by "What's the best way to invest this money so that I'm sure it will last?" "How long will it need to last?" "How much will I need to live on?" And these questions don't even approach the deeper issue of "What exactly am I going to do with all this free time and with what will be the last big stage of my life?"

Understandably, making all the decisions that accompany retirement and the money that goes with it is stressful, but it's also exciting. This portion of our massive transfer of wealth will pose some interesting challenges as well as enjoyable opportunities. Besides the difficulties of making good decisions for ourselves regarding an inheritance or a retirement plan withdrawal, this great transfer of wealth also raises issues of giving. It doesn't seem like it should be, but giving also can be complicated.

A third source of money in motion involves the elaborate and often perplexing procedure of estate planning. This process of deciding what's to happen to our money after our death can be very emotional. Once again the baby boomers are at center stage. The very individuals who will receive an inheritance from the older generation or who will withdraw from their retirement plans will also contribute to this transfer of wealth as they write their own estate plans. Money will continue to move as these and other members of our aging population distribute wealth to their heirs and throughout society.

It certainly seems like estate planning should be an easy thing to do: "Just divide what's left among my family members and make sure it's equal!" For many people, that will be enough, but estate planning has more potential for good than that. Everyone's situation is different of course and I'm not attempting to offer estate-planning advice here. However, it has always seemed to me that deciding what's to happen to our money beyond our lives is a golden opportunity to put our money to work in support of our values, our last chance to let our money represent what we stood for. And, unfortunately for some, it's also the last stab at domination, control, and abuse. With a well-thought-out estate plan, we can arrange to have our money speak for us in beautiful and eloquent ways after we're gone. But a poorly conceived estate plan—or worse, one that's drawn up in anger or malice or greed—will also speak for us, and it won't speak well.

Whether you're on the receiving end of the money in motion, the giving end, or both, money changing hands can be exciting. Most of us would like to participate, and, in truth, a great many of us will in one form or another. It's fun to think about all we will do when it's our turn to take part in this great movement of wealth, but what I've seen in many years of watching money change hands is that just below the surface of this excitement, there are other darker emotions. Right behind that excitement, there can lurk fear, anxiety, and greed.

The Paradox of Money in Motion

Despite all the potential for good and for growth, this money in motion will also be tangled up with the intense emotions of the very situations that set it into play in the first place. Inheritance, for example, can truly be a blessed windfall, but it can also be tainted by death or by the wishes and demands of the deceased. Retirement is what we all work toward, and yet it sometimes brings about a temporary crisis of identity. And so it is for many of the big financial decisions of our lives, which are either enhanced or diminished by the emotions in which we frame them. Money in motion is a complicated business, and we in the

United States are only just beginning to see how complicated it can get.

I do understand that the majority of us wouldn't view money coming our way as a bad thing. We're not accustomed to talking about the problems of having money, only the benefits. For obvious reasons, we focus much more on the problems of *NOT* having money than we do on those of having it. But there's a saying in the financial world that makes a good point: "When you don't have any money, all you think about is money. And when you have a lot of money, all you think about is money."

Money can be a full-time job. Managing it—making good decisions; putting it to work in meaningful ways; providing for families, friends, causes, and society at large—would be a tall order even if it could be performed in the absence of emotion. The problem is, of course, that financial decisions are rarely made that way. On some level, I think we all understand this. We certainly experience the two together when big decisions have to be made. But this relationship is something that we acknowledge very seldom. And even less do we pay attention to the great opportunity that lies behind this truth.

Money and the Turning Points in Your Life

Where then do we turn first in order to understand the role money plays in our lives and the ways in which it reveals our deepest selves? Fortunately for us, the ever-changing circumstances of our day-to-day lives provide ample opportunity to step back and observe.

It has been my experience over these many years of working

with people and their money that, although we deal with money every day, there are certain times when the money/emotion dynamic is more intense. These are the times when our lives are changing in some dramatic way, like retirement, divorce, or death. At these moments, our emotions will very likely complicate our financial decisions, and sometimes, believe it or not, our money will dictate our emotional ones. In these times, both the financial and the emotional stakes can be high.

It's around these major turning points in our lives that Part II of *The Value of Money* is organized. My goal in examining life events from the point of view of this money/emotion mix is to offer a sort of road map through the often-difficult sequence of financial decisions that each situation requires. I hope to highlight not only the concrete financial matters that must be tackled in each situation but also the emotional traps that often complicate our decisions. You will see the ways in which the different types of emotional relationships to money can play out in our decisions. And I also hope that you will embrace some of the spiritual lessons that can attend our money experiences.

Of course, everyone's situation is different, and so I obviously can't offer concrete solutions to personal financial problems here in this book. My goal is not to recommend any specific investment or financial strategy; instead the emphasis in *The Value of Money* is on the process of sorting things out, evaluating your situation, observing yourself in relation to your money, and then taking the proper steps in the proper order. The goal is that we better understand our money as well as ourselves.

But examining major life transitions from this dual point of view will also encourage you to dig a little deeper into your own life. Viewing your emotional makeup through the prism of your money offers you a chance to see yourself in a new and different way. And viewing your money through the prism of your emotions is also a unique approach to this important topic. These investigations promise many rewards, not the least of which is to make you a better financial decision maker. Even more important, they encourage a kind of awareness that can make us stronger, more compassionate, and more conscious. They invite us to examine the legacy we create and leave with our money not only through our spending but also through our deep relationship to it —our moncy consciousness.

3.

MONEY AND MARRIAGE

Money is probably not the first thing most couples think of when they contemplate marriage. Entering a new marriage ushers in such a time of promise and joy that the thought of financial matters might seem hopelessly dry and unromantic. This is a time when the future looks bright, and everyone is full of dreams. Money may in fact seem coarse and far too realistic for such a period of bliss!

While it's true that the nitty-gritty of money management is hardly romantic, ignoring it can cause problems that can most certainly drain the romance from a relationship very quickly. Money may not be the first thing a marrying couple thinks about, but it really ought to be somewhere on the list!

It seems to be stating the obvious to say that handling the financial issues of marriage in a responsible way is extremely important to the health and long-term prospects of your marriage. Experts tell us that money is one of the chief sources of disagreement within unhappy marriages. Of course, some couples slide gracefully into the financial decision making required in setting up a household. I suspect these are folks who have either an easy and realistic relationship to their money or have similar fears. Their styles match each other well and they're able to communicate about them.

But marriage requires financial compromises, and for some couples these can raise difficult issues. If people are unclear about their own attitudes toward money, if their relationship to money is a troubled one, or if their styles clash too dramatically, the normal financial challenges of marriage can become stumbling blocks to a peaceful relationship.

Just as entering into a new marriage is a time for joy and hope, it's also a time for honesty and openness and that includes the issues around money. Early on is the best time to lay a solid financial foundation for a marriage, to lay the groundwork for future financial peace and prosperity. At the very least, it's a time to begin to sort out money issues if any exist. Your future security and even your happiness may very well depend on it.

The Challenge of Shared Resources

Most of the life transitions discussed in *The Value of Money* involve rather complicated financial decisions. Even those that are quite clear-cut—like caring for an elderly family member, for example—have very significant ramifications for the people involved. By comparison, some of the financial issues involved in marriage—especially if we're talking about young people marrying for the first time—may seem quite simple. As is true in so many of our major life events, however, it's the emotional side of things that creates the complications. Bringing two households, two personalities, two sets of goals and needs, and two potentially different money types together can be a challenge.

Marriage is about sharing resources, and money is, of course, one of those essential resources that must be shared. For some people, just opening up their own purse strings to give another person access to their money can be frightening. Many people in our society shy away from ever letting anyone else even know how much money they have or earn, let alone give someone else the right to spend some of it! But marriage does require at least some of this kind of openness.

There's no denying the fact that, in our society, money is power. Who makes it, who has it, who controls it, who decides how to spend it—these are some of the power issues that surround money and that must be sorted out in a marriage. In the hopeful, romantic state of a young marriage, they may not be easy things to discuss. But discussing them is vital in the long run. They lay the groundwork for real cooperation down the road.

Rarely are things perfectly equal when it comes to the money in a marriage. Without some good communication, that inequality can pose a few problems. It's usually the case, for example, that one person earns more money or has the greater earning power in the long run than the other. (Traditionally, this has always been the man, but things are changing in our society and sometimes now it's the woman.) Should that higher earning give the earner more power over the money? Should that person have a greater say in how money is spent? These issues must be discussed. For the person who earns more, and thus carries the load of earning and providing, it can be quite difficult to allow his or her partner full access to the money or full decision-making powers. It's easy to feel entitled to a greater say in what happens to the money if you're the one who earns the bulk of it. By the same token, it's difficult to feel fully entitled if you are not the one who earns the money. Tensions can grow out of disparity in income. The same can also be true if one person comes into a marriage with more money or assets than the other. In fact, the issues of sharing, equality, and power come up over and over as married couples work out the best way to handle their money.

Friction Around Money

Beyond this major question of power sharing so important in a relationship there are all kinds of more ordinary issues around money that can cause friction in a new marriage. These things may have posed very little problem when you were single and handling your own money, but can suddenly become problematic as you work with your spouse. Spending patterns, for example, may be quite different if one person likes immediate gratification and the other is a saver. In this situation, there can easily be disagreement about the highest priorities for what to do with extra cash. To a saver, spending that extra cash instead of saving it may seem a waste or unwise. At the least, the situation will be frustrating. But to someone who enjoys immediate gratification and isn't inclined to put much money back, the saver must seem incredibly dull!

Longer-term goals can be quite different as well. Do we save for future children or a great vacation? Do we need to think about retirement or should we save to buy a home? A person who sees saving as a priority will immediately focus on these long-range goals and enjoy working toward them. But if his or her spouse has a different approach to saving and to money in general, these goals can easily be thwarted.

A good friend of mine always felt that irreconcilable money differences had contributed mightily to the demise of his first marriage. He was married to a wonderful woman whom he loved very much. But somehow he had entered into the marriage without really understanding how she handled her money. He was a saver if ever there was one. He loved to set a goal, put money aside regularly to meet it, and then took great pleasure in achieving the goal and making the purchase, whatever that was. He loved to count up his money, enjoyed thinking about it. He even made rather elaborate plans in his head about how he would handle his budget if he ever lost his job or got sick. He loved to plan, and planning around money was especially important to him. All of this made him very serious about his money and extremely responsible. Imagine his surprise when he realized he had married someone who couldn't have been more different.

For his wife, who earned far less herself, money was to be enjoyed. Life was to be fun, and to her, saving wasn't fun. She resisted any serious attempts at planning. In fact, she really preferred not to think about money at all and claimed that she simply didn't understand it. She liked to take whatever extra money was built up and spend it on something they could enjoy together. She bought all kinds of wonderful toys, like bicycles and things for their home. The problem was, of course, that she never discussed these purchases with her husband first. Some new object in their house or some new toy was constantly surprising him, and with each one, his frustration grew.

My friend realized that this was a very serious and deep rift. In his mind, it didn't bode well for their future. It scared him that he could never be sure about saving since he could never be sure that his wife wouldn't spend the money. He began to be more secretive about his money. She, in turn, took it very personally that he didn't seem to want to share with her or to enjoy their resources with her in the same way she did. Money wasn't the only reason that they parted ways after just a couple of years of marriage, but it was a large contributor to their unhappiness. It was a danger sign that they had completely missed in the early days of their relationship. It's sad, I think, that they were never able to talk this through. He might have been able to loosen up a bit and let go of some of his fear, enjoy his money a bit more. She might have become a little more responsible and learned from him how to set her goals higher and achieve more over time. It might have been possible for them to meet somewhere in the middle and each become better financial managers and a closer couple in the process. Instead, money—and many other things, I'm sure—drove them apart.

> When a "Wolf-Never-Leaves-My-Door" type marries a "Little-Lamb" type, there can be trouble.

Blending different styles of handling money and accommodating different longer-range goals aren't the easiest things to do. But they can be done if individuals are honest with themselves and each other and willing to discuss compromises. As is true with so many other things in a good marriage, it takes some good communication.

Opening Up About Money

Why is it that we're so hesitant to talk about money? This has always seemed odd to me but perhaps that's because I work so much with money and all of our emotions around it. But in our society, in general, people are still a bit reticent to discuss it. Couples may feel, for example, that it's unseemly to discuss such a crass topic as money with a new partner. Others may feel perhaps that there are problems in their behavior around money, so they want to hide these, especially at the beginning of a marriage when we're all on our best behavior. There may be a hesitancy to share our concerns about our partner's behavior around money or embarrassment about past mistakes of our own. For people who come into a marriage with significant resources, or for those with high earning power, there can be an understandable fear of being taken advantage of.

I think it's also true that many of us don't want to explore our relationship to our money too deeply for fear of finding some major malfunction. Opening up to our partner may, in fact, force us to acknowledge our problems, if any exist. Then, having revealed them to someone else, we would be compelled to deal with them. Getting real about money in our relationship might just be opening quite a can of worms. And in our society in general, of course, we're not encouraged to explore our relationship to money. Most of us talk far more openly about health issues or relationship challenges than we do about our financial concerns.

Yet there's no question that secrets about money can be damaging in a relationship, especially if there are some problems. This was most certainly the case with my friend. A little bit of honest communication goes a long way to heading off potential problems.

The interesting thing in all of this is that combining resources at the time of marriage can be the very event that propels you into a fruitful examination of your relationship to money. If you're unaware of your own money type, this may be the exercise that reveals it to you. For many people, I think, discussing attitudes and beliefs around money with another person, especially a person as important as a spouse, is a new experience, a new type of vulnerability. But working out the normal details of a household budget with another person, setting goals, combining incomes are just the normal parts of the financial side of marriage. It's an important part of your life together, and it may just show you things about yourself that you haven't suspected. Of course, these can be the discovery of some wonderful traits that you hadn't even appreciated. On the other hand, you may discover some things that need to be fixed!

Let me offer a few examples of some of the problem areas I have observed. On occasion, I've seen newly married people surprised by the difficulty they experience as they begin to share the resources that they've grown accustomed to enjoying all by themselves. The same income that they've been living on alone now becomes part of a joint income. The same money that supported one person now may need to support two people. There's lots of sharing that goes with marriage—that's for sure. Sharing your money may be something you haven't thought about much, and it can take some getting used to.

For others, it's the question of who controls what that can be quite difficult. For all couples, this is most certainly something that needs to be discussed and maybe even negotiated. Questions such as the following are all part of setting up your joint financial house:

- Do we want to put all of our money together into joint accounts, or is it better to keep some separate for each person's personal use?
- Should we divide up the bills and each pay according to our incomes, or should the normal household expenses be paid from money put together into one big pot?
- Who should actually pay the bills?
- Who keeps track of everything?
- How will we make decisions about extra expenditures beyond the basic ones? How will we set the priorities for extra money?

In other words, who controls what? Nothing will bring these issues of control and power that are inevitably part of every marriage to the forefront quite like money.

It's obviously very important to work out these details in order to establish a solid long-term financial relationship, and most couples do work through them in one way or another. I've seen over the years that there are lots of different ways to handle money within a marriage. No one pattern works for everyone. Some people divide their money up. Others put it all together. Some people have a very distinct "division of labor" when it comes to money decisions. And others just deal with each decision as it comes and take care of everything jointly. All of these different styles can work well. The important thing is to talk about it all from the very beginning, to keep talking about it as new circumstances arise and your life together changes, to know yourself in relation to your money, and to be flexible.

The Hidden Opportunity

Despite the fact that there can be challenges in dealing with money in a marriage, there is also great opportunity. What better way to explore our own basic attitudes than with another person whom we love? What better motivation could there be to understand and improve our relationship to money than our desire to form a solid and honest partnership with our spouse? Marriage forces us to consider our money in a new and different light. You are, after all, combining your resources with those of another person who comes to the relationship with a set of expectations that is undoubtedly as full as yours. Discussing the simple things like your budget is important. But even before that discussion, it can be interesting to ask yourself and your partner some basic questions that relate more to your emotions around your money than to the money itself. These are rather open-ended questions that could be helpful at any time in a relationship. But they can be especially useful as you begin married life. They can help you to get to know, not only your own money type, but also your partner's.

- Is there anything that scares you about sharing your money with someone else in general or with your spouse in particular?
- What type of expectations do you have for your money

and also your spouse's? Do you expect that the two of you will share everything? If not, why?

- What do you envision sharing when it comes to your money?
- Are there financial things you're hesitant to discuss? That you have some money hidden away for example, that you spend more than you would like, that you're afraid you won't be able to pull your own weight financially or that your spouse won't, that you don't feel you understand money too well or that you fear your spouse doesn't understand it?
- What are your priorities for your money?
- What are your fears?

Not all of these questions are appropriate for all couples, of course. And it's only fair that any question you ask, you must be prepared to answer as well. But these are the types of questions that get down to some of our emotional issues around money. Discussing these types of things reveals your financial personality to your spouse. The goal is to head off problems down the road, but in the process you might find that you become closer as a couple.

It can also be very useful to talk about your money experiences with your spouse, to share some of the past that has helped to form your attitudes and behaviors. How was money handled in your family? What money experiences make you feel most proud? Are there any you'd like to have a chance to do over?

This entire exploration is about understanding not only your own money type, but also that of your spouse. Just as individuals can have a specific type, so can a couple. As you begin to explore these questions that get at the heart of who you are in relation to your money, you can begin to form a joint money type that will be the foundation of how the two of you and your family will relate to money for years to come. This early stage of exploration is the beginning of a peaceful and joyful financial relationship or of a rocky one. It's the beginning of the legacy you will leave with your money as a couple and it can set the tone for many years and many generations to come. It's not only a helpful exercise. It can also be an enormously creative one.

On to the Decision Making

Once these more philosophical issues have been addressed, you and your partner can get down to the business of setting up your joint financial life. There are two issues to be tackled right away. The first of these is to decide who will have what responsibility. Who will do the banking? Who will manage the money—that is, who will make the day-to-day decisions on it? I refer here to such things as paying the bills and balancing the checkbook. In many households, there's one person who handles all of that. And if that's the case, how is the other person to access the money needed for ordinary daily expenses? In other households, it's a shared responsibility, or one person handles one set of responsibilities and the other another set. There's no one way of setting things up that's perfect for everyone. It's just a matter of deciding how you wish to arrange things and what will work best for you.

Beyond the "Who controls what" issues, there is the very practical and important step of setting up a budget. Establishing a basic budget is fairly simple. If you've been living on your own for a while, you probably know how to get started. The challenge will lie in the fact that now you're combining two households, two mind-sets, and two sets of priorities.

Budgeting is a matter, first and foremost, of knowing how much money you will have coming in and how much will go out to cover the expenses of your household. There are many simple spreadsheets available that permit you to list your basic expenses against your income. These are very helpful as you begin to make decisions on some of the essential things involved in combining two persons' lives. For example, once you know how much money you can spend on housing, you can decide where you will live. Once you determine how much is available for entertainment, you can decide how often you can eat out. Budgeting is a simple enough exercise. What's new about it in this circumstance may only be the matter of combining two personalities and two different points of view, of negotiating the priorities.

Another important step, once the basic budget is completed, is to begin setting goals jointly for yourselves as a couple. There may be more education that one of you seeks or a special vacation that you want to save for. Many couples begin thinking about children and putting back money for that exciting phase of life. And, of course, there's always retirement to consider. For all of these short and long-term goals, it's back to the budget to see how much can be set aside. The important thing, and perhaps the challenging part of the goal setting, is deciding together what the priorities are. You may find that money that's to be devoted to meeting your own personal goals must be shared with your spouse so that his or her needs, hopes, and dreams are also addressed. But budgets, just like investment portfolios, are flexible. They can and usually must address the needs of more than one person.

As a couple, you will begin experiencing the life events that form the basis of this book. Each new circumstance in your joint life, each new transition, will bring a new opportunity to evaluate and discuss your money situation. Most of the major life events considered in *The Value of Money* are transitions that can be shared as a married couple. The steps suggested in each chapter are exercises that can be done alone or together and can reveal an individual's money personality or that of a couple. As critical as it is to understand your own relationship to money, it may be even more important for the health of your relationship to understand your combined attitude or the ways in which your two belief systems work together. Tackling these major life transitions as a couple is the essence of a long and happy married life. And confronting them with financial self-awareness will contribute to the overall money legacy that you and your family leave in this world.

Marriage the Second Time Around

The reality in our society is that many of us will have multiple marriages in our lifetimes. Second, third, and even more marriages raise all of the same issues of combining different personalities and priorities that have already been discussed. But later marriages also raise some additional financial considerations that are quite different from those involved in a first marriage.

It's as important to understand your own relationship to money and that of your new spouse in a second or a third marriage as it is in an earlier one. Just as in a first marriage, decisions must be made about who controls what. Priorities for spending must be discussed and agreed upon. What is significantly different, though, in a later marriage is that each party may come to the relationship, not only with more significant financial resources, but also some very important financial responsibilities. There may, in fact, be quite a number of people involved in this marriage—from an earlier spouse to whom alimony is owed, to children from a previous marriage to be cared for and educated. The very fact that there have been earlier marriages can have a significant impact on your financial situation. It's essential to be open and frank about any financial responsibilities that carry over from that earlier relationship.

If either you or your spouse is paying out or receiving money such as child support or alimony, there may well be some strong emotion tied to that money. As is discussed thoroughly in the next chapter entitled "Splitting Up," divorce is an especially complicated life event from both the financial and the emotional points of view. There might be resentment and anger about this money or an uncomfortable sense of financial dependency on a person to whom you're no longer married. It's only fair to your new spouse to examine and discuss these issues and emotions. The financial and the emotional implications of your previous and ongoing responsibilities need to be understood and accommodated as much as possible.

But these are not the only types of complications that come up in a second marriage. Even if your children are fully raised, issues related to them and the family money sometimes arise.

Many years ago, I worked with a client whose husband had passed away after a long and drawn-out illness. Many years went by before she began to contemplate marriage again. She had taken such care of her husband for so long and she had loved him so much that she really didn't want to think about marrying again until a great deal of time had passed. But, eventually, she did begin to think about meeting someone else. She was not an old woman. She had many things she still wanted to do and to share with someone else, and she had the financial means to do them. She was ready to move on with her life.

The problem was that she had been single for some time and her children—all adults by then—had become accustomed to things the way they were. They thought of her as a mom and a widow. They saw it as their job to take care of her. They were as devoted to the memory of their dead father as she was and they seemed to feel that if she married again, it would betray that memory. But beneath all of those noble concerns, there was a less generous one. They were worried about the family money. Their mother was a wealthy woman. They all stood to inherit quite a bit of money one day. Although they would never have said it openly, they were concerned that if she married again, her new husband might receive the lion's share of her money at her death and leave them out in the cold.

I have no doubt that they were genuinely concerned about their mother and sincerely wanted to see her happy. But by the same token, they were also very concerned for themselves. They made each man their mother met feel quite unwelcome in their family and made it clear to her that they disapproved of her desire to find another husband. Sadly, she never did find anyone else. She lived out her years alone. And her considerable wealth went to her children at her death.

Family Protection

I don't mean to be too critical of this family. It's understandable to worry about a parent who looks to marry at a later age. And I know that financial issues can be a significant part of the worry. But in my experience, most couples who marry after their families are raised are very careful that their money be protected for the benefit of their own children. I've seen this done a number of ways, but most often it's arranged through some version of a "yours, mine, and ours" scenario. Usually, each member of the new couple keeps his or her money separate and then contributes to a joint fund by which they run their household, buy a home, travel, and do whatever other normal things they look to do together. But by using trusts drawn up by a qualified attorney or some other legal entity, both members of these couples set things up so that at their death, all of their assets pass to their own children. In addition, some couples add special provisions to these legal documents for the care of the surviving spouse if that seems to be needed. But then at that person's death, the remaining money passes to the spouse's children. The point here is that there are ways to set things up so that your money does pass to your own children from a previous marriage if that's what you wish, or to whatever cause you have selected. Chapter 10, "Controlling from Beyond the Grave," spells out in considerable detail many of the issues and opportunities that come up as you plan for the distribution of your estate after your death.

Marriage is about openness, compromise, discussion, and working together. This is just as true in the financial area as it is in any other aspect of married life. With a clear understanding of your financial beliefs and attitudes, with good open communication, and with a willingness to adapt and change things as needed, your married financial life can be very peaceful. It is for you both as a couple, as it is for you as an individual, a matter of self-awareness. But in addition, it's a matter of clear communication with your spouse and a kind of joint self-awareness that can be very creative. If using your money to express yourself is an exciting exercise for you alone, think how much more interesting it can be for two people working together.

4.

- -

SPLITTING UP

Of all the life events discussed in *The Value of Money,* divorce is one of the most complicated, both financially and emotionally. It involves a radical shift so filled with emotion and drama that many people can barely resist using their money as a weapon. But as much as we'll all hope to avoid divorce, when it becomes necessary it can present a significant opportunity for personal growth. Taking control of your finances in the challenging atmosphere of divorce can be a great stepping stone to a more peaceful and self-reliant life.

In my many years of practice as a financial adviser, I've seen a variety of emotional responses to the difficult issues presented by divorce. I've worked with individuals incapacitated by their pain, energized by their anger, reduced to childlike thinking, or hidden out in blissful denial. There are as many responses to this unfortunate situation as there are families enduring it.

When it comes to our money and our financial security, however, divorce is serious business. For many people going through it, there can be a great temptation to put off the money issues or to neglect some of the nagging details that can ultimately be very important. But decisions made at this time can have a long-term impact. They require clear heads, thorough analysis, and at least a measure of emotional distance, all things that are pretty hard to muster in the turmoil of divorce. The money side of divorce can cause panic, but, then again, if you're willing to approach it in this way, money can be the very thing to get you through it.

A Painful Reality with Great Potential

I remember a woman who was referred to me as she and her soon-to-be ex-husband finalized their divorce. After months of negotiations, she finally knew exactly what she was to receive and so was ready to get organized. Unlike many people in this situation, she seemed calm and self-assured as we sat down to review her settlement.

We began by talking at some length about how she wanted to live, what she wanted to do, and the new life that she was rather eagerly putting together for herself, but the more she talked, the more uncomfortable I became. It seemed, at first blush, as if there was a fair amount of money for her to live on. Her children were raised. She had a decent job, although it was not one she was terribly devoted to. The money she would be receiving was going to come from many different sources—retirement plans, IRAs, an old annuity, a little alimony, and proceeds from the sale of their small home—but, on the other hand, there was also a fair amount of debt to divide up, and she had completely ignored this side of the balance sheet. As I added and subtracted, she chatted amiably about all the things she wanted to do now as a single woman. I prepared myself mentally to deliver the bad news.

Simply put, there just wasn't enough money there to live the way she wanted to live. Sadly, she was going to come up very short. She had worked out lots of details in her head about what her new life was going to look like, but she hadn't consulted her financial statement at all to see if it could even begin to support her dreams. She was living in a fantasy, and I was the lucky person called upon to administer a dose of reality.

I checked and double-checked my numbers of course to make sure I understood her correctly. I asked more questions to see if, by chance, there was some more money that she hadn't remembered to tell me about. Then I delivered the verdict. She either had to find a way to obtain more money or find a way to need less. It was as simple as that.

She stared at me in disbelief, saying absolutely nothing. So, of course, I went on, explaining that she had several choices. She could, for example, look for a better-paying job. She could certainly postpone her retirement plans and continue working longer. She could consider trading down to a much smaller house for herself. And, of course, we could invest what money she did have in ways that would enhance her income, but I warned her that the increase would be modest. The truth was that, no matter what we did, she had some major adjustments to make.

With the blankest expression imaginable, she quietly gathered up her papers and excused herself. "I'll need to think this over," she said as she left my office.

I felt fairly confident that I would never see this person again. I figured that she would find an adviser who supported her fantasy instead of one who told her it wasn't possible, given what she was working with. She had been so enthusiastic about her new beginning when she came in that it seemed unlikely to me that anything would change. I felt bad for her: tough choices, and unhappy ones at that.

A few days later, however, she called and asked me if I would review her situation with her adult son, who lived in another state. When I reached him by phone, he told me that his mother had called him in a panic after our meeting. I was surprised. She had been so composed in my office. I hadn't been at all sure that she had absorbed what I had told her, but evidently she had understood my message completely. According to her son, she realized how unclear she had been about her options, and now that she was really thinking about her life, it had thrown her into a tailspin. Her son was asking if we could all meet to go over this whole thing again.

And so there was another meeting with this poor woman and her caring son. This time, the mood was much more serious. He asked lots of questions. She listened quietly, showing very little emotion. Once again I summarized for her a financial situation that presented more than a few challenges. They both thanked me and left.

Despite this second meeting, I still didn't imagine I would see this woman again. Somehow I thought that she might be a bit embarrassed about how unrealistic she had been or that she might not have believed me. Her situation wasn't a very happy one, but it wasn't the end of the world either. If she was willing to make a number of changes in the way she was living, completely revamp her proposed budget, and rearrange her plans for retirement, she would probably be fine. I just didn't think she wanted to.

But I couldn't have been more wrong. I had underestimated her. Behind that stoic expression and seeming impracticality were strong character, resolve, and the beginning of financial realism.

She scheduled another appointment with me, and this time it was her turn to talk.

When she arrived for our third appointment, I was happy to see her relaxed and cheerful. She pulled out a paper that detailed what she called her "new and improved budget." She outlined for me a number of changes that she had decided to make. She was going to find a less expensive place to live and she expressed willingness to work longer. She would curtail her spending and hold off on using any of her retirement money. Although it hadn't been evident to me earlier on, she had clearly understood the ramifications of her financial situation. She had decided to deal with them head-on and, in fact, went further. When we had finished our work together she lingered a moment in my office.

"You know," she said, "I guess I should thank you. I really hated everything you said to me about my finances. I wanted to believe you were all wrong at first. But then I realized it was true. I didn't have enough. I had to do something. For me, really, this whole situation is about stepping up and taking care of myself. I've always had other people to take care of me, and I've always let them. But not now. Now it's all about me taking care of myself. And this is where it starts."

> With determination and a dose of realism, a "Little-Lamb" attitude can become a happy "All-Is-Well" relationship to money.

It would be easy to say that this woman really didn't have a choice, that she had to step up to the plate and deal with her new reality, but that's not true at all. Many a person in her situation would have just gone out and found someone else to take care of them. Many people, especially those unaccustomed to it, would have resisted the responsibility she took on. But for this brave woman, divorce was about a new way of life. Her money or, more precisely, the lack of it provided a perfectly acceptable tool to use for standing on her own two feet, perhaps for the first time in her life. Her situation certainly wasn't a happy one and definitely not what she was hoping for, but she used it well to grow personally and in a direction of independence that she sought. I've never seen anyone move more quickly from a childlike relationship to his or her money to a mature one.

Money—An Integral Part of Divorce

Divorce is complicated in just about every way we can imagine. Even in the best of circumstances, the most amiable of separations, there's intense emotion and often tough choices. Finances are a frequent source of confusion. Understandably, for many people, the money issues become tangled up with their fears for the future, their anger at another person, or their concerns for their children. Or the exact opposite can be the case: The financial situation may reflect feelings of freedom, relief, and hope. As if all that were not enough of a burden, in the midst of all the emotions that surround divorce, there is often great uncertainty about the future. The uncertainty can be about lots of different things, of course, not the least of which is money.

It isn't possible to go through a divorce without focusing at some point on money. Because splitting up a household requires the division of assets as well as debt, money changes hands. Retirement plans and personal possessions get divided. Homes are sold or one person buys out the other. Business interests are split up. There's alimony to discuss, child support, and ongoing or future expenses like education for children. And then there is debt and all the responsibilities that go with it.

Going out alone as a single person, and especially as a single parent, requires a total rethinking of your financial situation. As couples work through the normal financial issues of a divorce, the decisions can be critical to the future security of everyone involved. I think sometimes that divorcing couples fail to recognize or admit the long-term impact of the financial decisions made at this difficult time. Facing that fact might make it all the more frightening.

Your new situation as a single person may require that you develop brand-new money habits, especially if you've had some bad ones in the past. Sometimes these bad habits go ignored when you're part of a marriage, but going it alone after a divorce will bring them quickly to light. This is a good thing, of course, but that doesn't mean that it's an easy situation to face.

Money, Divorce, and Your Future

Divorce requires you to think ahead about your money, to look down the road and try to determine what you'll need. This can be especially difficult as you try to imagine a completely new life or if you weren't the one who managed the money in your marriage. When you divorce, whether you want to or not, you take over full financial responsibility for yourself and perhaps for your children as well. From setting up and holding to a day-to-day budget, to retirement and estate planning, you're now in control of your finances.

Some unproductive behavior is understandable. The whole matter of money can be quite daunting when you're in the middle of the turmoil that divorce causes. In fact, for many people, divorce is more about looking backward than looking forward. But divorce is a time when you must set the stage for your future. In a situation that can often feel very out of control, money is one area where you can take charge. As unpleasant as it might seem at the time, getting control of your financial life throughout and after a divorce is a positive way to shape your own future. For some people, like my client who eventually took control of her own financial life, this circumstance drags them into a more mature relationship to their money.

Of course, not everyone has a difficult financial situation to deal with as they divorce. You may not be working with less money. In fact, you may be working with more. Many of the people I work with are assuming responsibility for a great deal of money as a couple's assets get divided. The challenge may not be adjusting to a lower standard of living at all. It may be taking control of a large sum of money and learning how to manage it. The challenge may be more about understanding what you have and what to do with it than anything else. Of course this is a much happier situation, but to some it can still feel like a burden, especially if they're unaccustomed to such responsibility. Although it may feel like a challenge, it really isn't that difficult a task. With a little study and some good advice, everyone can get a handle on his or her financial situation.

Money as a Weapon

Because money is such a big part of divorce and because divorce is so filled with emotion, many people can't resist the temptation to use their money as a weapon. Unfortunately, it's too easy for some couples to use the division of their money as a place to play out the emotional drama of divorce. The press is filled with stories of angry celebrities who fight endlessly over their sizable fortunes, but sadly the amount of money doesn't really seem to matter. Many a couple has gone to the mat over small amounts of money in an effort to express their anger or their hurt, punish each other, or relieve their frustration. Some feel they deserve more, especially if they're not the ones who initiated the divorce. Others try to hide money to avoid having to divide it. Many people hold money over their partner's head in order to get something they feel they want or need. "Give me what I want, or I'll fight tooth and nail for all the money." It's an understatement to say that divorce is a time of hurt feelings and anger.

Fortunately, not everyone lashes out in anger and pain. Many of the couples I have assisted in this process have behaved quite amicably. For instance, I received a call from a couple I had worked with for a few years.

"Hi, Susan. It's Jim. Becky's on the line as well. We need to talk to you for a moment. We are getting a divorce."

I was caught off guard by Jim's relatively lighthearted tone as he delivered the sad news. But it quickly became apparent to me that Jim and Becky were determined to approach their divorce in the most positive way they knew how. They had decided on it together. They were trying to plan the next phase of their lives.

They were friends during their marriage, and they were surely going to remain friends after. Division of their financial assets and liabilities was quick, fair, and generous from both sides. Although their separation and divorce seemed unusually easy, I suspect that there are many people who go their separate ways peacefully without lashing out at each other or causing pain. It's just not what we're used to thinking of when we think of divorce.

 Money has no intrinsic power.

For those individuals for whom the intense emotion of divorce rules the day, however, the temptation to use their money irresponsibly can be quite hard to resist. But there is good news: Just as this temptation to use money as a weapon can be compelling, so too can the desire to overcome that temptation. Seizing the opportunity to use money as a stepping-stone to growth and personal responsibility in this difficult situation can be just as compelling and, obviously, far more rewarding.

Money and Empowerment

Taking over the management of your own money as you step out of a marriage and into life as a single adult is a very empowering step. Getting real about your money—evaluating it honestly, making decisions as objectively as possible, and treating it as a tool and not as a weapon—is the hallmark of a mature and healthy relationship to money. For people going through a divorce, there are multiple opportunities for adopting a mature approach. There are simply many layers of money considerations to tackle. And, in fact, the money decisions themselves can help a person through a divorce. I'm happy to say that over the years I've seen many people use the new money responsibilities that come with divorce as their first step toward an independent and happy life, the means by which they begin to get back on their feet.

Divorce is all about struggling for independence or perhaps being pushed unwillingly toward it. Whether you really want to be independent or not, if you're going through a divorce, you're going in that direction. It may not be a responsibility one savors, but it's a vital component of your future security.

Tackling the Money Issues

I've worked with both men and women as they've gone through the various stages of divorce. That is to say, I've worked with both parties, the one initiating the divorce and the one who may have been surprised by it. When divorce comes up, most people first are overwhelmed by their own raw emotions. They worry of course about their children. Money may not be the first thing they think about, but it will likely be very high on the list. The money issues that come up and the way they're handled depend a great deal on who is initiating the divorce. As the division of assets unfolds, one party usually considers him- or herself the giver and the other the receiver. In truth, both are giving and receiving. It's in everyone's interest that both parties give and receive honestly, generously, and fairly.

Sometimes a client will seek out financial advice very early in the divorce process. These are usually the people who are initiating it. They're wondering what the financial issues are, and, frankly, they're calmly evaluating the financial ramifications of their decision. In the best of all possible worlds, they're thinking it through for both parties. In the worst, they're trying to understand how much financial damage divorce will cause them. It's not unusual for a financial adviser to know about a person's decision to divorce before the spouse does.

Other people seek out financial advice somewhere along the way but before the divorce is completed. In this case, they're often tying to evaluate their status before it's locked in. At this point they may have a pretty good sense of what financial resources they will have once they're divorced, so they're beginning to get organized. Or they may have decisions to make, such as buying a new home. Often one of the first discussions I have with a divorcing individual is about how much money he or she can put up for the purchase of a home.

Finally, some individuals evaluate their money situation only after a divorce has been completed. With the divorce behind them, they're often ready to get on with their lives. Some tackle the money issues with gusto as they move forward. Others go about the whole thing with a begrudging acceptance of a new reality. And I suspect there are those who refuse to engage with their money at all, whose pain is too great or anger too intense. For them, the money issues must wait until other, more pressing needs are met. Some come with their lawyer or CPA, some come with their friends, and some even come with their ex-spouse. Some are relieved and joyful, others depressed and angry. Many are exhausted. Some are organized and businesslike. Others are simply looking for someone to take care of them. But all are there because they have important decisions to make.

As hard as it can be to think clearly and rationally when you're tumbling through a divorce, that's exactly what you need to do when it comes to your money. As common as divorce is today, it's still a major life emergency when you're the person going through it. Everything else takes a backseat to this incredibly disruptive process. In fact, for those going through a divorce, there's very little about it that isn't serious. And that's especially true when it comes to your money. Despite all the emotion and high drama involved in divorce, you must still make decisions, especially money decisions, with a clear head and a certain amount of detachment, realism, and flexibility. It's not always easy to gather the strength for the kind of objectivity it takes to honestly evaluate your situation, but it's important to try. It's equally important to work with an adviser who guides you in that direction.

Getting the Financial Lay of the Land

So what do you do if you find yourself in this unhappy situation? Where do you start in order to get a handle on your finances and what your financial future might look like? As is so often the case in a major life transition, the first step is to get the financial lay of the land. You must analyze your entire situation from a financial point of view. At a time like this, many people have so many things on their mind that money gets lumped in with everything else. Of course, this is an understandable reaction to the dramatic changes going on, but it's a good idea to devote a little time specifically to your money. There are many things that need to be sorted out, things that may well influence everything else.

The first step is to ascertain exactly what money you will

actually have once you're divorced. It's helpful to *make a list of all assets that you will be receiving.* It's also very important to know in what form the money you receive will be as well as in what type of account. In other words, will your money be in cash, or will it be already invested? Will you have access to it right away, or will it be tied up in a type of account where you can't necessarily get to it immediately (in retirement plans for example)? Often people receive money in a divorce settlement that comes to them over time. Will yours come to you all at once, or will you be receiving it in installments? If it's coming in over a period of time, like alimony payments or child support, for example, will it remain constant or decrease over time? When will it end? (These types of payments generally taper off as your children get older.)

Undoubtedly you will have some combination of all of the above. Ideally there will be money available to you immediately (like in a savings or checking account) as well as some long-term money that may have a few restrictions on it (a retirement plan, for example). Considering both short-term and long-term money gives you the freedom to deal with your immediate needs but also to begin to think about your later financial security.

In addition to your share of savings and retirement accounts, you may receive other sums: your share of the equity in a jointly owned home, for example, or your share of the proceeds of other assets sold off, like a vacation home, a farm, or personal property. There could also be other payments included in your divorce agreement that you won't see for a while. You may be entitled to a share in your ex-spouse's pension plan, for example. That could be a payment that you won't receive until he or she reaches a certain age. Or you may receive a portion of an ex-spouse's social security or a portion of an unusual payment like a special severance packet if your ex-spouse takes an early retirement. These are all things to be taken into account as you begin to plot out your financial future and anticipate your needs.

All of this list making is simply getting the financial lay of the land. What you are trying to understand here and spell out as clearly as possible is exactly what you will have immediately, what you will have at a later date, when you will receive each piece of your financial puzzle, and any restrictions there might be on your money. From here you can begin to see what gaps there are, if any.

Understanding what you will have, however, is only one part of getting an accurate picture of your financial landscape. Now we come to the second part of this initial planning stage. Money coming in is one thing; money going out is another. Just as you need to know what you have, you must also evaluate what you need. The best way to do so is to *draw up a budget.*

Even if you're staying in your home, you will need to rethink your budget. Many people, however, do not stay in their own home and must set up a new household. Drawing up a new budget can be quite challenging. It may have been some time since you've done this for yourself or perhaps for yourself and your children. Not only can it be challenging, but it can also be a bitter pill. It isn't uncommon for every line in the budget to be a reminder of pain, anger, or sadness. Nonetheless, it's important to determine what your expenses and financial responsibilities are going to be and to try to do it in as realistic and objective a way as possible.

And now, the third part of this "Lay-of-the-Land" stage of evaluating your finances. Here's the $64,000,000 question: *Does the money you have or will receive plus the income you are bringing in from all your various sources cover your needs?* If so, you're in good shape. You can relax. If you have extra money above and beyond that, even better. You can begin to think in the long term and plan for your future.

If your income doesn't meet your needs, however, you must go back to the drawing board to reevaluate your situation. Are there expenses you can reduce? Do you need to consider less expensive housing? Can you do a different kind of work that pays more or can you supplement your income in some other way? Adjusting a budget from a two-person household to a one-person household or from a two-parent household to a one-parent household isn't easy, but it can be done. And this is the type of compromising that's required. It demands, of course, that you be realistic about things like the size of home you can buy or the amount of rent you pay. It may require that you work more or spend less. All of this can be very emotional, unhappy, and unpleasant, but it can also be an opportunity to really evaluate what's important in your life. Nothing reorganizes your priorities like a financial shortfall!

I've seen clients truly embrace this stage of taking control, as was certainly the case with one of my clients, Carol, a woman who had led a very lavish life while married. With divorce came the dilemma of a much-reduced budget. She certainly had enough money to live on but not nearly as luxuriously as before. Rather than hating her new situation, she embraced it. She thought long and hard about what was important to her in this new phase of her life. She was willing to compromise on just about everything except for one thing. She had decided that she couldn't live without her beautiful garden. So she set about finding a house that needed her skills! Finally she found the perfect spot: a very cute and affordable house with a large yard that just begged for the kind of garden she loved. She made this little house her own, gardened to her heart's content, and never looked back.

 Money is the bridge between our values and our material world.

There's a trap in this early stage of planning that's easy to fall into. In an effort to get settled and comfortable, it's tempting to think only about your past and throw all of your money into coming as close as you can to replicating your old life. Many people try to afford all the same things, live in the same neighborhood, and generally maintain their old lifestyle. That may work fine in the short term, but it might also jeopardize your long-term security. As important as it is to get yourself established in order to move on with your new life, it's also important to think long term. Whatever you set up at this early stage must be sustainable. Once again, a dose of practicality is needed.

Many people do, of course, remarry, but I believe it's a good thing to make your financial decisions assuming that you will be responsible for yourself for the rest of your life. This encourages you to look down the road as far as you can and understand that, just as you need money now, you will also need it later. As you begin to live your life as a single person, it's important to make sure you're not digging too deeply into a nest egg to meet current expenses that could, in fact, be reduced. Long-term financial planning is always a bit of a juggling act. Suffice it to say here that you must keep the long view even as you're pushing and pulling to adapt to the short one.

A Word to Women

Divorce is challenging for both men and women to be sure, but I would like to add a special word here to women. It seems to me that in our society men are better trained to step up and take care of themselves financially. Many women still view this world of money as a strictly masculine domain. It can be especially challenging, therefore, for some women to step into this role of financial decision maker. (And I believe equally difficult for men to assume other roles that women accept more easily.) For some women, it's difficult to think beyond the incredible tangle of emotion that divorce brings up in order to calmly contemplate fending for themselves financially. Often enough, I see women simply throw up their hands and say they don't understand.

Well, it's one thing to not be interested. Many people just aren't that interested in money. But it's quite another to say you can't. You can and you must! Divorce thrusts that responsibility upon you. The good news is that getting a handle on your money can be a path to more than just financial independence. It can lead to greater independence overall. It may be that you really don't want that independence, and that's fine, but from a financial point of view, you simply must take the reins for yourself. To shrink from that responsibility is dangerous; the stakes are simply too high. Fortunately managing your own money isn't rocket science.

Much of what a good financial adviser does is to educate. I've often advised people that if they don't understand their adviser, they're probably not working with the right person. Likewise, if an investment seems incomprehensible, it's probably not a good choice for you. Working with a good adviser to design, implement, and monitor strategies for your money is something you can do. You might even discover that it can be fun.

Once you have gotten the financial lay of the land and, if necessary, adjusted your current living costs to the new reality of being single, it's time to think longer term. Now we're on to Step 2 on this road to financial freedom.

Planning Your Financial Future

You cannot assume that the planning you did with your ex-husband or ex-wife will work for you alone. Although some of it may still apply, it's best to start over and plan again, this time thinking only of yourself and your children if you have them.

Now is the time to *think about your longer-range goals,* like retirement, and to determine what you will need at that later stage of life and how you will meet those goals. You can go about this quite systematically, determining what you'll need, when you will need it, how much more you need to save to achieve your goal, and even whether or not your goal is realistic. The steps spelled out in Chapter 5, the chapter on retirement, can guide you in evaluating your longer-range situation and show you how well you're doing. Once you have determined what your goal is and how much is needed to achieve it, you can set about the task of systematically working toward making it a reality. This is basic financial planning, and it's extremely important for a person embarking on a newly single life. It can spell the difference between a secure future and one that's filled with uncertainty and fear.

Taking Care of the Children

If you have minor children at the time of your divorce, you must also give thought to the difficult scenario of *what would happen to them in the event of your death*. Is there money available to provide for them? Is there life insurance money that would fund their future needs? Who would be responsible, first of all, for their care and, second, for managing their money? Who would you trust to use your money for the purpose you intended on their behalf?

To that end, it's very important to *spell things out through an estate plan* drawn up with the help of a qualified attorney. What are your priorities for your children in terms of upbringing, education, and the like? How do you want your money managed for them? Let me give you an example of what I mean by this as it pertains to the money.

If your minor children would receive a significant amount of money upon your death (think of the total of your life insurance, personal property, brokerage and bank accounts, and retirement plans), you would need to designate someone to be responsible for managing it. You would need to communicate to that person your thoughts on how you would want the money distributed to them. At what age, for example, do you wish them to take over the management of their own money? Is all of it for education or are there other things you would like to see funded? Are there restrictions you would place on them regarding their education, things like public versus private education, distance from home, and type of study? Of course these are issues that married parents of minor children must deal with too, but they take on a special urgency for the single parent. It's best if everything is clearly spelled out in print. You need to think through as many of the issues as possible and discuss them with the person who will be managing the money in your absence. Accepting that responsibility is a serious commitment. You should make your wishes as clear for him or her as possible.

In addition to that, a newly single parent should automatically update not only wills and trusts but also *all beneficiary information.* Individual retirement accounts, life insurance, annuities, pension plans, and employer-sponsored retirement plans all permit you to list your beneficiaries. These are the people to whom those monies automatically pass at your death. If your ex-spouse was your primary beneficiary in the past and you now wish these accounts to be passed to your children, you must update your beneficiary designation on each of those accounts. Stating it in your will does not suffice. You must complete a new beneficiary form for every such account and make it quite clear by dating it that it's an undated declaration. It's easy to forget this little detail, but it's very important. Negligence here can have a significant impact on your children if something happens to you. These monies pass to whoever is listed as the beneficiary. If you have failed to name your children, then they will not receive the money. More than once, I have seen money that should have rightly gone to one person go to another simply because a divorcing parent never updated his or her beneficiary information.

Getting Invested

So now you've evaluated not only your current needs but also your longer-term ones. At last it's time to actually *invest the money* you are now controlling. Fortunately, all the work you've done up to this point makes Step 3 a much easier task.

If your analysis shows that you need to invest some of your money for current income, you may take a more conservative and income-oriented approach to your investments. If, on the other hand, you have no need for current income and you wish to focus more on future goals, you might take a more aggressive and growth-oriented approach. Or your analysis may show that you actually need both: a bit of income now but also some growth to meet future needs. For some people, many in fact in this divorce situation, it may be the other way around. You may need your investments to produce some growth now and then income at a later date when alimony or other payments taper off. The important thing to understand is that it's the analysis of your needs that will strongly influence the direction of your investments—your needs and your emotions.

As you begin to invest your money as a newly single person, pay close attention to your emotions, because there will undoubtedly be some. Investment literature and some advisers might tell you that you need to put your emotions aside in order to be a good investor. And it's true that a certain amount of detachment is vital to the evaluation of your needs and the management of your investment portfolio. Calm rationality helps keep investors from being too shaken up by the day-to-day gyrations of the stock and bond markets, which really have very little to do with long-term success.

But that's quite different from being aware of and acknowledging your emotional reaction to the decisions you're making. An aggressive growth portfolio might be appropriate for you, given your age, your goals, and your net worth, but, if it scares you to death, it isn't right for you. You may not need current income from your investments, but if the stability and predictability of a high-quality bond portfolio is the only thing that allows you to sleep at night, then your portfolio should likely be tilted in that direction. If you try to understand your fears about your money and you can articulate them, then you can take them into account in the design of your portfolio. Fear of loss, of not having enough either now or later, and of volatility can easily be addressed and assuaged in a good investment plan.

At every stage of your process, it can be very helpful to work with a competent and trusted adviser. Good advisers can help you not only to quantify your needs but also to verbalize your concerns. Once taken into consideration, your adviser can help you allocate your money in investments that have the potential to take you in the directions you need to go. Your adviser can also help you with another very important element in your financial picture, the *ongoing monitoring of your money*.

Once a portfolio is up and running, the hard work is mostly done, but it still needs to be reevaluated on a regular basis. This is not to say that it needs to be redone or that you need to start over, but you do need to stay on top of it. On a regular basis—I believe at least every six months and certainly any time there's been some major event in your life—you should take a hard look at your investments with a few questions in mind:

- Does the original allocation between growth investments and income investments still make sense? Does it still meet my needs?
- Is each component of this portfolio doing its job? Am I experiencing growth from the portion that's growth oriented? Am I receiving adequate income from the income side?

- If a portion of my portfolio is not performing well, why not?
- Do any changes in my life require a change in my strategy?
- Am I on track in meeting the goals that I set? What is my progress? In other words, how am I doing?

Being forced to take control of your finances because of a divorce is, I believe, a hidden blessing in disguise. If you can see it in this light, then perhaps this one part of the whole unpleasant divorce experience can be a gift. At the very least, it's an opportunity to cultivate a better relationship to your money. It may be a more mature and responsible one if that's what's needed or simply a more deliberate one. It can and should be a source of pride. Even if the news isn't good, facing your financial picture square on can be the beginning of getting your life back on track.

It's hard to avoid some sadness throughout a divorce, and finances often contribute to that sadness, but how you handle your new financial reality is up to you. The potential for good is there. Despite all the anger, fear, sadness, and confusion that divorce can bring up, there is at least that one silver lining.

5.

- -

RETIREMENT

Of all the life events that financial advisers counsel their clients through, retirement is certainly one of the most significant and the most anxiety producing. For the majority of people making this life-changing transition, the stakes feel very high indeed. First of all, there's a confusing array of decisions that must be made, many of which feel irrevocable. In addition, what most people would consider a large amount of money often changes hands in retirement as distributions are made out of retirement plans. Finally, the most significant part of our earning years comes to an end once we retire. For better or for worse, we begin to live off the money we've saved. Even individuals accustomed to making financial decisions on their own often seek help when it's time to retire.

And yet retirement is something many of us dream about. It's the freedom we work toward, the golden years we all hope for. It's that opportunity we seek to do what we want, at the pace we want, and where we want. As scary as the actual step into retirement is for most of us, it's also a time of great excitement and promise. To say the least, it's a highly emotional time, and the money decisions don't make it much easier.

The First Tentative Steps

There's no question that from a financial point of view retirement is one of our most important life events. We should expect it to be emotional; it's a big decision. But I think we often ignore the extent to which the emotions that so many of us feel can color and maybe even dominate our financial picture.

The retirement of one family member affects the entire family. It's a change in everyone's routine, not just the actual retiree's. I've seen wives of retiring men who are far more nervous about their husband's retirement than the men themselves. In fact, I've seen spouses who haven't been in the workforce for some time step out to find a part-time job when their partner is about to retire! The idea of both of them rattling around the house is just too scary!

As difficult as this change can be for family members, for the person who is actually about to enter this new phase of life, retirement can cause enormous anxiety. It represents a complete change in lifestyle and can, in fact, bring on a sort of temporary identity crisis. The biggest question on everyone's mind of course is, "What am I going to do with myself?" Work provides most of us with a pretty firm structure to our days. Retirement is virtually without structure or at least can seem that way at the outset.

I've been surprised over the years that we don't give more thought to this aspect of retirement. Perhaps the process of actually retiring—making all the financial decisions, training a replacement at work, finishing up tasks, leaving friends and coworkers—is all that a person can handle. Many seem to feel the rest will take care of itself. Perhaps this is good; a lack of structure after so many years of work may be just the thing to usher in a whole new phase of life. But when I ask clients what they see themselves doing in retirement, most people can't think beyond the first few months. Women will often talk about what projects they want to undertake in their homes. In fact, it seems to me that people's homes do provide a good transition into retirement. Many a long-awaited home remodel has eased a family into retirement.

Travel too is a major theme. I've seen clients plan the trip they have always dreamed of or hit the road with no real destination in mind. Some even sell their homes to live in a mobile home for a year or two while they see the country.

And then there are those who plan nothing but wait to see what comes to them. They give themselves a period of time to do whatever they wish. They get up when they want, read whatever they like, work in the garden or not. They have coffee with friends, do a little volunteer work, and catch up on old movies. They rest awhile, and then, after some time has passed, a sort of routine emerges for their new retirement life.

All of these approaches are good ones, of course. They're all responses to the tremendous change in life and in identity that retirement necessitates. It simply takes time for people to settle into a new life, time to work through all the emotions of this period, and time to adjust to a new money reality.

Take my client Judy, for example, who found herself retired quite suddenly because of downsizing. Thrown into retirement by a major corporate shake-up, she literally was given no more than a day's notice. She was shocked, angry, hurt, and disappointed.

Fortunately for her, she had always had a very clear head when it came to her money. She knew exactly what she needed to live on, and she knew exactly where all her money was. It was a good thing that she had such an easy and graceful relationship to her money. It made the financial decisions that she was called upon to make rather quickly much simpler. This was important since the emotional struggle she faced because of the way she tumbled into retirement was significant.

 An "All-Is-Well" relationship to money can make a traumatic change easier to bear.

Her financial decisions might have been easy, but what to do with herself was quite another issue. She was paralyzed with confusion. She had worked for so many years that the only thing she could think of was to get another job, maybe just part time, to give herself a little breather. So she focused her attention there. But somehow, almost without any reflection, the part-time job never quite materialized, and she found herself gravitating toward some projects in the community. None of this was planned; it just unfolded. Today she's as busy as she wants to be, helping school kids who need a little extra help, volunteering at a hospital, and reading for the blind. Nothing turned out the way she would have predicted, but it all worked out beautifully nevertheless.

I also remember another client whose situation was quite different. This fellow had a shop behind his house that was his favorite spot. Because of his hobby, he was more ready to retire than most, and so the decisions were relatively easy for him. His eyes were on a very specific reward: free time to work in his shop. He told me that on the day he actually retired, he came home, walked in the front door, and went straight through the house, out the back, and into his shop. He was a happy man!

A New Relationship to Our Money

There are as many ways to handle the transition into retirement as there are people making it. But I believe it's safe to say that, for most people, there will be anxiety at some phase of this major life event. It's simply a very emotional change.

For obvious reasons, a great deal of the anxiety about retirement gets focused on money. It's true that there are many very important money decisions to be made. But beneath those obvious concerns, there is another more abstract one. For most of us, retirement requires a major change in our relationship to our money. We are called upon to take control of it in a way we might never have done before. For years we work toward retirement. We save and we earn. We're always (hopefully!) putting money away for the future. But as we enter retirement, that future is here. Our earning years and our saving years are largely over. Everything we've done to get to this point of retirement must now pay off. If we haven't done what we needed to do, if we haven't saved enough, our retirement dreams may be compromised. Even if we have saved enough, we now must step out on faith and live off those savings. It would all be quite easy, of course, if we knew exactly how long we were going to live. But we don't, and so the "Have I saved enough?" question looms large. The answer to that one question alone will shape our retirement activities.

For many people, one of the most difficult parts of all of this is the actual decision making that surrounds the retirement itself. There are a million things to consider, it seems, and all of them important. Beyond the huge issue of "What will I do with myself?" there are the equally important issues of "Do I have enough money?" "How much will I need to live on?" and "How long will my money last?" If one is given to worrying, everything about retirement can be potentially worrisome.

And yet, throughout all, there is excitement. For many people, most perhaps, retirement is a wonderful phase of life: a time of change, freedom, new possibilities, and long-awaited rewards.

The Turmoil of Decisions

Over the years I've seen lots of different reactions to all the turmoil of this decision-making stage of retirement and many different ways of handling it, some better than others.

There are those who research and research and research until they're barely able to sort through the stacks of articles they've accumulated. There are those who simply do what their friends have done—a very risky approach to these important decisions. Some are quite ready, of course, and they tend to take the decisions in stride. Because of other interests and activities, they move quickly and gracefully into their new life. Others can only make this break slowly. They prefer to retire in stages, gradually weaning themselves from their work routine and transitioning into a new and more leisurely life. They break the decision making down into more manageable pieces. Of course the way we approach these decisions will have a lot to do with the emotions we're feeling as we make changes. And the way we make all these changes is predicated on our emotional relationship to money in general.

Sooner or later, retirement decisions will come down to the money. To step off into retirement without fully evaluating your financial situation would be both foolish and dangerous indeed. And here's where our emotions come into sharp focus. There are so many fears that routinely surface.

For many people, there's a very real fear of no longer receiving a paycheck. When you work for your money, you have at least some sense of control. You feel you're "earning" it and you can earn more if necessary. In retirement, however, you're no longer "earning" your money to the same extent. For many, this is a frightening loss of control.

Some people fear that there won't be enough money to last an entire lifetime. Of all the goals that clients have regarding their money, this one, of not outliving one's money, is the most common. Retirement puts that goal into sharp focus. As you plan your retirement years, you are very clearly planning for the rest of your life, right up to the very end. None of us knows when that end will come, and so we don't know how much money will actually be needed. Running out of money in old age is a very frightening thought!

The financial decisions necessitated by retirement can seem startlingly irrevocable. Although most are not, a few are, and so many people are very fearful of messing them up. Understandably they fear making a mistake that will undo all their hard work of so many years. I've never seen anyone make so poor a decision as to completely ruin their financial lives, but I have seen people make some bad ones that do make a difference down the road.

All of these fears can be addressed as you structure your finances to support you in your retirement life, but, quite frankly, there's no substitute at this juncture in a person's financial life for some clear thinking and a little soul searching. With an honest and objective evaluation of one's emotional state as well as one's financial situation, retirement can open the door to the freedom we all dream about. Freedom to do what we wish and to express parts of ourselves that have gone unexplored during our work life. Or freedom to develop some part of our lives or ourselves with more attention than we were able to devote while we were working. Once you're past the hurdles of all the initial decisions and with a solid financial strategy in hand, retirement can be a wonderful time of life.

The most intense work that financial advisers do as we work with retiring individuals occurs at this all-important decision-making time. We see people at their most nervous, uncertain, vulnerable, and excited all at once. We see spouses and partners just as nervous about all the changes taking place. But I'm happy to report the following very common occurrence.

In early meetings with a person entering retirement, we talk through all of these issues, so that a client can make decisions and implement a plan based on a strategy we design together. There are many phone calls, questions, conferences, and adjustments to new circumstances. Then six or eight months later, a retiree will come back to my office to review the plan to see if any tweaking is needed. I can report that, almost without exception, people look happier and healthier a few months into retirement. They look more relaxed and certainly calmer. They seem well rested. And they've almost always become involved in interesting activities of one sort or another. One of the most common comments we hear from our retired clients is, "I don't know how I ever had time to work!"

Accommodating Emotions

Plans for the future, fears and concerns, expectations, financial realities, and needs—these are the things that we discuss with an individual about to retire in our initial meetings. It's as important to get the emotional lay of the land as it is to get the financial one. Over and over I've seen that an investment strategy or financial plan may match up well with a retiree's financial goals but not with that person's emotional relationship to his or her money and thus be doomed to failure. Let me offer an example.

Let's imagine that you fear stock market fluctuation. Your greatest priority for your money is to conserve what you have. Your greatest fear is to not lose what you've managed to save, but at the same time you're retiring rather young, and your parents and grandparents have lived long, long lives: You're a young retiree with great longevity in your family. Your financial adviser will look at that long life expectancy and know that growth is an essential ingredient in your investment mix. Your investment portfolio may need to work for many years well past your actual retirement date. He or she may well recommend that a portion of your money be placed in growth-oriented investments, perhaps in the stock market. But this is to ignore your greatest fear, since stock investments can fluctuate in value. Although this strategy may match your need perfectly, it doesn't match your emotional temperament at all. If, on the other hand, the only investments used were the most conservative ones (to address your fear of loss), there could be a different but very real danger. The lack of growth in the portfolio could leave you high and dry, without adequate income, many years down the road.

The good news is that the investment world is filled with alternatives, and there are numerous ways to provide growth and at the same time minimize risk. Sometimes it's a matter of altering the investment choices. Other times we try to work on the fears. The important thing though is to understand what all the needs are at the outset and then to systematically address them. And by all the needs, I mean both the emotional and the financial ones.

Sources of Anxiety

So if you are approaching retirement, what's your greatest fear? Here are some of the most common ones that my clients have discussed with me over the years.

The first of these and by far the most common is *running out of money* and being dependent on family, friends, or the state. No one likes to contemplate such a situation, and many people consider making their money last them their whole life a gift to their family. They may not be able to leave an estate, but if they're able to take care of themselves to the end of their life, they have done something for their children.

Another common fear is that of *making an irrevocable mistake.* I think it's only natural that, as we make all our retirement decisions, we fear making an error that will cause irreparable harm. The decisions are important and at times seemingly monumental, which is all the more reason to take a calm and informed approach to the whole process.

Many people also have a fear of *being taken advantage of.* Again, this is understandable. The details of our retirement decisions can seem somewhat confusing, and it certainly helps to work with a trusted adviser. But if you have never worked with anyone, you may fear that you're not choosing the right person to rely on for guidance. It's worthwhile to take the time to find out as much as you can about the adviser with whom you're considering working. Any good adviser is happy to provide you references and plenty of information on his or her past experience.

It comes as no surprise that some people fear *being overwhelmed* by the responsibility of all the financial decision making. If you are one of those people who avoids financial decisions, you might find this responsibility exhausting. Although the fact that you get to retire at the end of them is often reward enough to keep even the most unwilling decision maker going. Again it helps to work with an adviser who can walk you through the process and to be as systematic as possible. And there's no substitute for getting an early start on your planning when it comes to retirement.

It goes without saying that making decisions on your money can bring out a fear of losing money and jeopardizing your own future as well as that of your family. In fact some people seem to fear more for their families than they do for themselves. Retirement really is in lots of cases a family affair.

Losing a predictable paycheck is another common source of anxiety. Most of us base our household budgets on the flow of income that we've gotten used to over our working life, but retirement can change that flow rather dramatically. If this is a concern, it can be addressed in the investment strategy you design and a regular "paycheck" arranged for.

And finally there is concern about *having enough money to do the things that you have dreamed of doing in those "golden years."* Most of us dream about all the things we would like to do during retirement, most of which require some money. So it's understandable that we might worry that we won't have enough to enjoy our retirement years or that if we spend our money on those things we've dreamed about, we won't have enough money to last an entire lifetime. This may sound like a catch-22, but in fact it's not. It's usually very easy to accommodate these types of intermediate goals in the design of a good financial strategy. The key is being able to articulate what you want and also being able to put a price tag on it.

In fact, all of these concerns can and should be addressed in the design of an investment portfolio. The important thing is first of all to acknowledge what your concerns are and then to discuss them, to discuss not only your fears but also your hopes and ambitions.

Three Stages of Retirement

Retirement actually has roughly three stages. Most of us tend to focus on the first stage, the one during which we get to do all the things we've imagined ourselves doing once we're no longer working. These are the early years of good health and high energy, often referred to in our industry as the *"go-go" years.* I have found that most of us plan fairly easily for how much money we'll need in these years. Once we settle into retirement, we know what activities we want to fund and what it costs to run our home.

But there are at least two more stages of retirement that require our attention. After these "go-go" years comes the stage when we're beginning to slow down, the *"slow-go" years.* For many of us, these years will require less money. Our health may still be pretty good, but we may be staying closer to home, doing fewer things, and thus spending less money.

And then there is the third stage, for many the most expensive one. This is the oldest stage that we tend to resist thinking about while we're actually in the midst of making those early retirement decisions. This is the stage that is, for most of us I believe, the most frightening: the *"no-go" years,* when we may require assistance, even nursing-home care. This period often constitutes the most expensive phase of our retirement years. It's not uncommon for families to need a significant amount of money at this time. For many, there are high medical expenses and, if one person in a couple requires a nursing home or assisted living, the need to maintain two households. No investment strategy should ignore this stage of life. I believe there should always be a portion of the plan dedicated to providing for these years.

There are so many things to think about as you make the transition into retirement. The emotions of the change itself, the challenges and opportunities of hard-won freedom, the complications of a variety of financial decisions, the very real need to conserve assets for a later stage that can easily be thirty to thirty-five years in the future—retirement can be confusing!

Sometimes one set of considerations may seem to cancel out another, but in fact, with good planning, clarity, and a little objectivity, a sound investment strategy can easily encompass a wide variety of goals and priorities. It can even address those that transcend the retirement years and enable an individual to leave a lasting mark through gifting, family foundations, or special trusts.

Despite all I have said about the anxiety involved in making retirement decisions and about the challenges we face, retirement is a wonderful opportunity to make life meaningful. For many, it's the first real opportunity to do exactly what we wish. No matter what your goals are during this stage of life, there will undoubtedly be some sort of financial side. Proper attention to money at the early stage can provide the freedom and also the security to make all the years of retirement peaceful.

Years Before You Retire? A Few Simple Rules

How then do you begin to organize yourself for this major transition in your work and personal life? For starters, a great deal depends on the number of years before the actual retirement is likely to take place. Ideally you have a few years during which to prepare. Many employers organize some kind of meeting or series of meetings designed to help employees think through their retirement. They invite professionals like myself to discuss the financial issues, representatives from health organizations to talk about health concerns, speakers from a wide variety of volunteer organizations, educators on social security and Medicare, and former employees now enjoying retirement. These meetings are a great service; they motivate employees to think about all the right questions and they go a long way toward relieving some of their anxiety. On top of all that, they're fun. These meetings encourage people to begin serious preparation, but, even more important, they also encourage them to think about the potential of retirement years, potential for enjoyment and for contribution.

So let's assume that you have several years before you actually retire and you're now taking stock of your situation. Good for you! Here are a few general rules to guide you on your way:

Pay Yourself First

The first thing to realize is that you must save money. Retirement won't just take care of itself. There are many vehicles out there through which to save, but for most people a great place to start is with their employer's retirement plan. I often tell clients that their company's 401(k) [or 403(b) if you work for a nonprofit organization] is the first line of defense in saving for retirement. This is because, once you begin, your contributions will be automatically deducted from your paycheck. In addition, they'll come out of your pay before tax and so will reduce your current taxable income. Finally, and best of all, many companies provide some kind of "match": This means that if you contribute a certain amount, your employer will contribute a set amount on your behalf. There will always be a vesting schedule on your employer's contribution (meaning that you must remain on the job for a certain period of time before you can take that money with you when you go), but it's still a terrific boost to your account value. If your employer doesn't have a retirement plan available, you may begin your own investing by contributing to an IRA. These too can be set up to be funded automatically. IRAs also offer tax advantages and a wide variety of investments to choose from. The key is to get started!

Sometimes younger people tell me that they can't afford to contribute to a retirement plan. If that's the case, then you must start small and increase your contributions over time. Something is better than nothing, and you may find that you can adjust to the change in your budget rather easily.

Others resist saving, saying that the contributions seem so small that it hardly matters. But it does matter; over time these amounts grow. You add a little. Your employer adds a little. If the money is well invested within the plan, the markets may add a little too in the form of interest or dividends or growth. The key is to just get started and let time work for you.

If you would like to contribute more but don't feel you can afford it, get started with whatever you can manage. Then, whenever you have an increase in pay or with each New Year, increase your contribution by a little until you've reached your maximum. Retirement investing, especially when you're young, is a long-distance run, not a sprint.

Let Retirement Money Grow

When an emergency arises, it's often tempting to borrow from your retirement plan. As you pay the money back, you're essentially paying yourself, and this is often the argument for dipping into a retirement account to satisfy a current need. It's true that you are paying yourself back, but your accounts can still suffer quite significantly as a result of your loan. At the end of the day, your retirement too will suffer because your accounts were robbed of two important elements: earning power and time in the markets. It simply isn't the best place to take from. It's usually far better to keep retirement money invested and to let it grow.

Think Twice Before You Cash Out Your Retirement Plan

In today's economy, employees change jobs far more than used to be the case. For a younger employee changing jobs, it's tempting to simply cash out a retirement account and take the money (and pay a big tax bill at the same time). But once again this is very shortsighted. These monies can be transferred to an IRA or to a new retirement plan with very little fuss and remain tax deferred. Your preparation for retirement remains uninterrupted. If you cash out your plan, you must start all over again. You've lost not only money but also valuable time.

Invest with a Plan

Setting up systematic contributions to some sort of retirement plan is a great first step toward future security, but there is more. Once your money has been contributed to a plan, you must direct the investments within that plan. Here is where many people get confused. It's worthwhile to spend some serious time with your financial adviser or with whatever type of assistance your employer provides to determine what's best for you.

An excellent way to do this when we're talking about a 401(k) or 403(b) is to work with the materials provided by the company sponsoring your retirement plan. Employers often provide a sort of worksheet that walks you through a series of important questions related to your age, your goals, and your investment temperament. These worksheets are designed to help you define how aggressive or how conservative you need to be. They're not meant to make your decisions for you, only to guide you as you make your own decisions.

Stay Diversified

Once your money is invested it's extremely important to spread it out. It's never a good idea to pour all your money into the one thing that has done the best, assuming that it will continue to be the best performer. We never really know for sure what the next big winner will be. Remaining broadly diversified means that you will participate in the gains if any area of the market goes up. It also means that you won't be as hurt by losses should one or two areas go down. Diversification offers a measure of protection against bad markets and participation in good ones.

See Your Retirement Fund as Part of a Larger Strategy

My final rule for managing your retirement-plan investing is one that far too many people ignore. It's that one extra step that can help organize your financial life and give your portfolio's performance an extra boost. It's a step we often facilitate for our clients. Not only is it simple to do, but it also gives you a sense of organization, an overall strategy, and a measure against which to evaluate the performance of your investments as time passes.

Look at your retirement plan as one piece of a larger puzzle, one slice of your financial pie. Frequently I see individuals choose the investments in their 401(k) or their 403(b) with little or no attention to their other assets. They end up with a great deal of overlap among their different investments, or too much concentration in one thing. And, often, employees don't really know what they have in their company retirement plans. More than once, I've had clients tell me that they don't own any stocks at all, but when I've looked at their retirement plan statement, it showed otherwise. It's vital to know exactly what each option in your retirement plan really is, and then choose each investment carefully, making sure that each part contributes to the overall strategy.

When you look at your investments, think of your whole financial picture: your retirement plan but also IRAs, savings, and all your other financial assets. Make each piece of this financial puzzle work together. Make every piece do its job. For obvious reasons here, it's helpful to work with a knowledgeable financial adviser who can help you sort through your many choices and understand the potential of each investment.

Retirement Imminent? Steps to Take

These rules are fine for those who have many years until they actually retire, but what of those individuals who are now close to retirement and beginning the actual process of decision making? Once again, some simple planning can ease the pain and anxiety that so often accompany this major life event. To lay the groundwork with some good planning is extremely important because when we reach this stage of things, it's harder to separate our financial decisions from our highly charged emotions.

After many years of working with people who are making this passage into retirement, I've observed that the questions that need to be addressed can be grouped into three categories. Each one takes us more deeply into our finances as well as our emotions, until we can bring our money situation in line with our hopes for this last stage of our life.

The first category, which concerns day-to-day life, is a fun one.

Here you ask yourself questions that relate to the things we fanta-size about as we look forward to retirement:

- "What do I want to do with myself?" (new activities, favorite hobbies)
- "Which of my current daily routines do I want to keep?" (coffee with friends, early-morning walk)
- "What will I have time to do now that I always had to put off?" (exercise, reading, writing)
- "What will I miss and what won't I miss?" (old friends, stress)

It's fun to contemplate the possibilities, which are what many of us think of when we imagine ourselves retired. But most of us get to the second category of questions quickly, and it's often our money that leads us there.

Because retirement represents such a significant change in your relationship to your money, this is the time to honestly observe the feelings it provokes. Ask yourself, first of all—and answer as frankly as you can—what your greatest concern is as you move from living off a regular paycheck to living off your retirement savings. Is it that you won't have enough money to last your life-time? Is it that you fear a cataclysmic event will leave you without resources? Or is it perhaps that you're afraid to make decisions affecting your money, that you feel ill prepared or uninterested? Whatever it is that you feel, you're not alone! We all experience some strong emotions when we take on these big decisions, and these emotions absolutely dictate how we handle a major event like retirement. We may not care to admit it, but these emotions will play a major role in our transition into retirement. Even if thinking about our fears doesn't alleviate them, acknowledging that we have them will make us better decision makers.

This may all sound somewhat grim, but in fact it isn't. A good investment strategy should address all of an investor's concerns. If, for example, you're afraid of running out of money, emphasis can be placed on conservation. If your concern is reproducing that regular and predictable paycheck, a portfolio can be structured to generate regular income that will feel like a paycheck. If the idea of regular decision making is an unpleasant one, then a strategy can be designed that is simple and "self-propelled." The important thing is to know what's most important to you and to understand thoroughly and express honestly your concerns.

Of course it isn't all fear that we feel around our retirement. Although most people experience some kind of anxiety, most also understand the tremendous opportunity that retirement offers. This brings us to the third category of questions, which go to the heart of who we are and what we want our mark to be in this life.

Most of us spend a great deal of our lives meeting the expectations of others, but in retirement—assuming we've planned our money well and gotten through that initial period of adjustment—we have an especially clear opportunity to shape our own lives. Many of us experience a freedom that we haven't had for some time. But unlike when we were young and heading out into the world for the first time, now we have experience and hopefully some wisdom. In retirement we get to contemplate what it is we really wish to do while we still have time and health. What is it we wish to leave behind? For what would we like to be remembered? In some ways, these retirement years can feel like our last chance to do or to be what we've always dreamed.

Opportunities

Many times I've been inspired by the ways in which my clients have grown into their retirement. Once they have passed that initial uncomfortable stage, they settle into a routine that very often includes doing more for others than for themselves. Volunteer work, teaching, new careers in the nonprofit world, family or community projects—these are the types of things that many retirees find rewarding. And once again there are significant financial considerations involved in any one of these endeavors.

Let's say for example that your dream is to fund a scholarship at your favorite college or university. Your investment portfolio can help you make that happen. Or perhaps you long to teach your grandchildren about some exotic land. Your investment portfolio can finance such a project. If you'd like to build houses for those less fortunate, your portfolio might just buy you the freedom you need to do so.

> Money is the bridge between our values and our material world.

At every stage of your life, your money will play an important part in the fulfillment of your dreams. But retirement might be the stage where you can most easily press your money into the service of your dreams and priorities. If not at this time of your life, then when?

Getting Down to the Nitty-Gritty

Once you've explored your feelings regarding retirement and the concerns you might have about your money, it's time to get down to the business of evaluating your actual financial status. It's essential as you enter retirement that you know exactly where you stand. Although it might seem a daunting task at first, the truth is that this process is not as difficult as you might imagine. Answering a few basic questions will enable you to get organized and understand exactly where you are financially, what's already in place, and what still remains to be done. The following four questions are the place to start.

1. How Much Money Do I Have? If you've never done it before, now is the time to take an accounting of everything you have. Make a list of all your assets, where they are, what they're worth, and what exactly they're made up of. Include everything: retirement plans, IRAs, deferred compensation, employee stock ownership plans, annuities, certificates of deposit, savings accounts, checking accounts, mutual funds, savings bonds, life insurance, long-term care insurance. Leave nothing out of this financial inventory.

When you go through this process, you might be surprised to find that you actually have more than you thought. Our financial lives are often rather helter-skelter. Such consolidation, even if it's only on paper, can be very heartening. Over and over, I've witnessed how surprised my clients are when they see it all lined up on a single sheet of paper. It's very often more than they thought.

2. How Much Do I Owe? Just as you need to know exactly what you have, you must also take into account all that you owe. Once again, make a list of every debt you have. Consider your mortgage, car loans, educational loans, home-equity lines of credit, personal loans, and credit card debt. Tabulate each amount owed, who the lender is, the interest rate you are paying, and when you expect to have the loan paid off.

Hopefully, at this stage in your life, this list will not be long. Going into retirement with heavy debt can be quite danger-ous. Fortunately, most individuals reaching retirement age have reduced their debt to very little or to a very manageable amount. If you have not, you must look hard at the wisdom of retiring.

3. How Much Will I Need to Live On? For many people, there is very little change in their expenses when they first retire. It's a good idea to consider this issue nonetheless. There may be some new expenses for special projects like travel or a hobby. By the same token, there may be some decrease in expenses related to work, like transportation costs. But it's important to know exactly what you'll need to assure yourself that you'll have enough coming in. Although it would be difficult to know exactly how much you'll need thirty years in the future, at least you can evaluate the near-term and make a few assumptions about what will be needed later.

4. What Will Be My Sources of Income? Here is the all-important list. What money will you have coming in from the various sources available? The answer to question 3 has told you what you need. The answer to question 4 will tell you if you'll have it. Once again, you need to make a clear list that includes social security income; pension income, if you're eligible to receive it; income from other sources, like rental properties or mineral rights; income from any ongoing employment; income from your various investment accounts; and military retirement.

I often encourage clients to draw up this list excluding any income they might receive from an investment portfolio. In this way, the list can begin with those items that are potentially predictable, like a pension and social security. From there, it's easy to see if there is a gap that must be filled by investment income. This will be a major issue as you begin to design your investment strategy. The design of an investment portfolio for a retiree often begins with this question of how much income the portfolio must generate to meet current needs. If no income is needed, a portfolio can be structured to provide more growth for a later time. If current income is needed, taking care of that immediate need becomes the priority.

What Every Retirement Portfolio Needs

With these four questions answered, you can begin to set the priorities that will dictate the type of investment portfolio you need. Based on your goals, you will have a clear sense of what that portfolio needs to do: provide growth or income, conserve your nest egg, provide for another after your death, leave an estate, meet a special goal, and so on. Here you will want to work closely with your investment adviser as you work out the strategy or strategies that will meet all your requirements.

Investment portfolios can be surprisingly flexible. They can and often do address a variety of priorities. It's not at all uncommon, for example, to design a portfolio for a couple whose financial temperaments are completely different. We can build a plan that accommodates the conservative and the aggressive alike. But there are a few basic components that retirees should look for in their investments: income, liquidity, diversification, and growth.

Ideally your portfolio provides what's needed immediately while still preserving something for the longer-term needs that are harder to predict. Obviously a portfolio must provide the *proper amount of income*, especially if current income is needed. If that's the case, a segment of your investments will need to be structured to generate regular and predictable income.

But *growth* is equally important. As we're all living longer and as the cost of living continues to rise, it may be that you will need more income later on. What is sufficient now may well be insufficient when you're older and must deal with the high cost of health care. It's that growth portion of the portfolio that you may need to draw upon at a later date when your situation might be quite different. Balancing the elements of income and growth is very important and must be regularly monitored. This begs the issue of asset allocation.

Many investment professionals feel that the most significant contribution to the success of a portfolio is the proper balance between stocks and bonds—the *proper asset allocation*—and yet many investors pay very little attention to this important element. There's no one-size-fits-all solution here. You must discuss this balance with your financial adviser, taking into account everything this chapter has already described. Too often investors weigh their portfolio down with too much of one thing, often an investment that's done quite well in the past, thereby dramatically increasing their financial risk. But having the right mix of stocks and bonds, of conservative and aggressive, of income-producing and growth-oriented vehicles provides an investment portfolio with balance and, hopefully, a longer and most fruitful life.

Liquidity is also an important element in any portfolio. Most of us feel quite uncomfortable if we don't have some money that's readily available. Liquidity is important not only in an emergency but also when you need to adjust your portfolio for some special need or to take advantage of other investment opportunities.

And finally, there is *diversification*. As tempting as it is at times to concentrate our investments in just a few names, it is generally wise to stay diversified. This means that you own a wide variety of investments representing different industries, areas of the market, and parts of the world. Likewise your bonds should come from different issuers and offer varying maturity dates.

It's easy to argue that you might make more if you put all your eggs in one basket, and that is true if you pick the "right" basket, but you'll also lose more if you pick the "wrong" one. In my experience most investors, especially retirees, would sacrifice some of that potentially extraordinary growth for balance and a reduction in volatility that wide diversification offers.

Each of these components—income, liquidity, diversification and growth—is important within investment plans, but they're especially important as you enter retirement. You have no idea how long you'll need your investments to provide for you. Your portfolio should be flexible. It may need to be quite the workhorse!

Tough Choices

There are times when financial realities force retirees into some tough choices. One of the greatest conflicts arises when an individual requires more income than a portfolio can safely produce. This is a rough situation to be in. Are you spending too much? Do you have too much debt? Is retirement really possible at this time? If you find yourself in this predicament, you must do some careful planning in order to prepare for and deal with this situation before you actually retire.

If you feel you might fall into this category of investor, take heart. It is possible to find a compromise in the conflict between your current need for income and your future need for growth. It's a delicate balance to be sure but one well worth maintaining. Ultimately the important thing is to be extremely realistic about your situation and to think beyond this early stage of retirement to a later stage that could be very expensive. This may mean taking less income during those early years than might seem ideal in order to invest some money for later. Or it may mean continuing to work part time into your retirement in order to supplement your various sources of retirement income. And for some, it may mean postponing retirement for a few years. In any case, without the careful planning that ought to precede that step into retirement, the risks of a big mistake are far greater.

At other times, however, spending more than a portfolio can produce is the mark of a troubled relationship to money. People who do this spend away happily with very little regard to what they're actually earning. It always amazes me when individuals are blind to this situation. They draw heavily on a portfolio but seem completely in the dark as to how much their investments actually produce. They seem confused and surprised by the drop in value that's almost inevitable in this situation. And many times they find it all but impossible to change their spending habits.

However, sometimes these individuals are able to get a grasp on their finances once they realize what's happening. That was certainly the case with my client Marie, who became so realistic and courageous about her money once she looked at it straight on. But often enough they simply continue to draw their accounts down, ignoring the long-term risk to their security. Occasionally individuals get angry with their financial advisers even as they're drawing out far more than the portfolio can possibly earn, draining their investment portfolios. Their future looks grim.

The Opportunity of Retirement

In the best of all possible worlds, this review of your finances as well as your emotions and goals will uncover plenty of money, very little debt, and a strong and confident mission for your retirement years. Ideally, there will be no financial hurdles to overcome. In this case, normal anxiety will give way to excitement and enthusiasm about all the possibilities the freedom of retirement offers. For many people, this is exactly how things work out. The principal challenge is not finding enough money to live on in retirement; it's deciding exactly what you want to do with your new freedom and the rest of your life.

Thus retirement is an excellent opportunity not only to get your financial house in order but also to begin to contemplate the ways in which your money can become a part of the legacy you leave (much more on that later). It's quite valuable to begin this reflection well in advance of your actual retirement, at least two years before you anticipate retiring and maybe much earlier. It serves not only to clarify your thinking about a stage of life that might well last thirty to thirty-five years but also to pinpoint any problems in your financial plan. I've often seen individuals go through the process of taking stock simply to assure themselves that they're on the right path. When an opportunity to retire does present itself, they know quite clearly if they're ready to take advantage of it or not. Even if they choose not to retire, having thought the whole thing through gives great peace of mind.

Retirement can and should be one of the most exciting transitions in our emotional and financial lives. If we properly prepare ourselves in both these areas, our retirement can afford us the freedom we've worked so hard to achieve. It's a period of life that can be filled with new discoveries, vast opportunities, and great reward.

In retirement some of my clients have started new businesses, traveled the world, devoted themselves to important causes, engaged in new ways with family and friends, taken up new hobbies. They have gotten healthier and happier. They've experienced themselves in new ways in the world, and in so doing they've enriched not only their own lives but also the lives of all those around them. They love retirement!

6.

BECOMING THE
FINANCIAL CARETAKER

One of the fastest growing segments of our population is the elderly. As a nation, we're living longer and healthier lives than ever before, and this simple fact has begun to change the profile of our entire society. From health care to family dynamics, from real estate to the development of a whole host of new products and services, we're adapting to this new growth in our society in all kinds of interesting ways. It should come as no surprise that longer life, especially longer old age, has massive ramifications for your money.

The Financial Challenge of Growing Old

Financially, our longer life expectancies present a challenge that begins well before we reach old age. Living longer in retirement means that your money must last longer, that your investment portfolio will need to provide for you for a very long time. Even if you draw up a financial plan when you're quite a bit younger—in fact, especially if you do it at a younger age—you must seriously consider that all-important last stage of life. This may mean that your portfolio must incorporate more growth, balance more risk, and sometimes even sacrifice immediate needs to provide for longer-term ones.

In the old days, financial planning assumed a relatively short life after retirement. Today, an individual retiring at sixty-five may, in fact, be looking at a retirement that could last twenty-five or thirty years. Lasting that long, retirement can be a time when new careers are forged, new projects undertaken, and new relationships developed. It's full of promise and potential, and it's definitely a time when our money must work for us.

When we think about retirement, we tend to focus on the stage when health is good and we have lots of energy to expend. It's the retirement we all dream about: one filled with fun activities, freedom, and leisure. The harsh reality of our longer life expectancies, however, is that eventually we will decline and begin that last stage of retirement when we may become dependent on family and friends and most certainly will be involved in the health-care system. That decline can be a very significant development within a family and a dramatic change for the person requiring care, of course, but it's also significant for the person being called upon to give that care. For every elderly family member who needs assistance, there is someone being asked to provide it.

This dependent stage of life is the stage that financial advisers worry about the most. It's complicated in just about every way we can think of, but most of all it can be very costly. While our newly retired clients focus on the fun stage of their retirement, the phase that often includes travel, time with grandchildren, hobbies, and friends, we financial advisers are also thinking about that "down-the-road" stage when many of these activities are over and more money is needed. Money must be available for this period of life. It must be in order. And, in some cases, there must be quite a bit of it.

The Money Issues

Most of us think about this dependent stage of our lives or the lives of our parents in terms of day-to-day living— staying in one's own home, getting around, driving a car, and managing medications—but we could easily add money management to this list of considerations. There is, of course, the major issue of having enough money to cover all expenses, but there's also the business of managing it: how to invest it, how to know how much is needed, how to organize it to generate the income that's required, how to protect it from those who would take advantage of the elderly. These are just some of the issues that the elderly must face.

Most of us are aware that the last years of life can easily be the most expensive phase of retirement. Medical bills are often quite high. Medications can be expensive. In the case of couples, one of whom requires assisted living or a nursing home and the other remains independent, two households or living arrangements must be maintained. Some people need assistance in their own home and must navigate their way through the often-confusing array of resources in their community. Many elderly people, if not most in this type of situation, also need someone to help organize and orchestrate their daily life. This responsibility, which generally falls to a younger family member, can be quite a challenge.

In the best of all possible worlds, these tasks are carried out with grace and care. Hopefully family members have already discussed these matters, and the elderly family members have made their wishes known. Much heartache and worry can be avoided if families work together before a crisis arises and talk about what might be needed and what type of arrangements are available and/or affordable. What type of care do parents prefer? In their home? Assisted living? Where would they like to live? Near their children? With their children? What resources are available in the community? What are the parents' financial resources? If these details can be worked out or even just discussed before decisions need to be made, some of the emotional struggle of caring for an elderly parent can be alleviated. Sometimes it's just a matter of overseeing what our parents have already put in place, but that's in the best of all possible worlds.

Unfortunately, however, sometimes the caretakers are starting from scratch. When no preparations have been made, it's a matter of arranging an elderly person's life as best one can with very little input from the person most affected. There can be an enormous array of decisions to make, none of which will seem that perfect. Dealing with the emotions of the elderly person for whom you're making decisions isn't the easiest thing either.

The Emotional Challenge

Few life events that involve the complicated tangle of money and emotions are as charged as this one. Taking over for our elderly parents, or allowing our children to take over for us, brings up a tremendous number of emotional issues on both sides. Getting older is, as my own mother likes to quote, "not for sissies!" And watching our parents get older is no fun either.

Most of us would say, I believe, that taking over for our elderly parents is an onerous task. We're sad to see them decline; the job itself is demanding; the decisions can seem so irrevocable. Both the older and the younger generations shun the situation, but, like so many other important transitions in our lives, this one too provides plenty of opportunity for growth. Many people do accept this elderly stage of life with grace, and many caretakers are guided only by love and compassion.

No matter the circumstances, however, taking over for our elderly family members is a delicate job. At times, it can be hard to recognize that the time has come to step in. We resist acknowledging it because we don't want to. Even if we do see the decline, it's hard to know how much help is needed, and it's hard to offer it in a graceful way that allows our parents to maintain their dignity.

I well remember the time many years ago in my own family when I received the first signal of the very early stages of my father's decline. Our whole family had gathered for an event, and we were headed back home after dinner. My older brother quietly asked my dad if he wanted one of us to drive for him since it was dark. My dad agreed and, in fact, seemed quite relieved. I was shocked. It had not occurred to me at all that my dad might be having trouble driving at night, but clearly both my brother and my father were aware of it. That was my first sign that Dad was beginning to lose some of his earlier abilities. It hadn't even dawned on me that I needed to watch for ways to help him. I remember thinking that day that our family had entered a new phase.

In some family situations, it's very hard to take over for a parent. It can't be easy to be graceful as we allow someone else, even someone whom we love and trust, to take charge. And many younger family members resist taking charge, not wanting to take on the role of parent to their parents. It's a reminder, of course, not only of our parents' mortality but also our own. Understandably, there can be a great deal of resistance on both sides.

In many ways, making decisions for our parents can be harder than making them for ourselves. Financial advisers see this all the time when clients take over the management of their parents' finances or when elderly clients must bring their children into their deliberations. For many younger people in this situation, the stakes can seem very high and the person for whom they're making the decisions extremely vulnerable. There's almost always some level of fear about making mistakes.

When we make financial decisions on behalf of a younger person, there's usually time to recuperate or change things if we make a mistake. With elderly family members, however, we don't have time to recover financially from a mistake, and, perhaps even worse, we don't want to be the one who jeopardizes our parents' financial security at this delicate time of their life. So much of our investing and our financial planning is predicated on some future goal. In the financial care of the elderly though, we're dealing in the here and now, and the people for whom we're caring are often the people who cared for us. There can be a great sense of urgency and responsibility.

I once worked with a family whose story showed me not only how complicated this situation can be but also how much potential for growth and grace it has. This family was forced to deal with the grief of a powerful father's decline and, at the same time, his fierce anger at that decline. Some of them ran from the challenge of his painful descent, but one family member used it as a springboard to improve her relationship to money and to cultivate compassion.

Leslie's Story

Leslie was a woman my own age who had been my client for many years. I thoroughly enjoyed working with her. As is the case with my best clients, I had worked with all aspects of her financial life, had met several members of her family, and had gotten to know her quite well. She spoke freely to me about her work, her own children, and her extended family. Leslie's parents were elderly and, because she had always been a very active investor and took a great interest in all things financial, she had begun helping her parents with their money. This was a wealthy family whose situation was a bit complicated. I worked closely with them and connected them with other professionals to help them get their affairs in order. Over the years, we adapted her parents' investments to each life change.

First they bought a home nearer one of their children and then, eventually, moved into a retirement complex. They began a program of gifting to their church and to their grandchildren. They even funded a small scholarship for students who wished to study science. I spoke often with various family members about different aspects of this constellation of family accounts.

One day I received a call from the patriarch of the family. He and I had spoken often, and he had always been very astute when it came to money matters. This day, however, I noticed that he kept mixing up his numbers. Ten thousand dollars suddenly became one hundred thousand. When I reminded him that we were talking about ten thousand, he seemed a bit embarrassed and confused. "Of course," he said. "It's ten thousand. What a difference a zero makes!" His joking barely concealed how hard he was working to keep it straight. This was my first glimpse of what the family had been dealing with for some time. Although physically healthy, mentally he was deteriorating each day. Leslie and I began to discuss this health crisis in the family. Each time we spoke, she would give me an update on a story that had no possibility of getting better.

Eventually, Leslie and her mother took over all the financial dealings for the family. This was, of course, the easy part of dealing with the father's decline; there was plenty of money to care for him and for all the rest of them in fact. With no financial worries and health matters under control as much as possible, the greatest challenges involved the emotional issues, and this was a family filled with emotional issues.

Leslie had many brothers and sisters scattered all over the United States, each of whom tried to help in his or her own way, but inevitably the lion's share of the day-to-day work fell upon one family member, Leslie's brother, who lived closest to their parents. He had a very difficult job. This man and his wife were the ones who were called out in the middle of the night each time help was needed. It was they who had to listen to their father's complaining as he became more and more confused and unhappy. And, as is so often the case with this type of situation, their efforts to help were viewed as intrusive by the one needing the help. In their father's mind, this one son simply couldn't do anything right. The older man was unhappy; he wanted things to be the way they had been twenty years before. He ranted and raved. He yelled at them and said terribly hurtful things. A lifetime of anger seemed to come out of him. To others who came to visit, he was most cordial, but to this one son, most hateful.

The people who could see this happening assured them all that this was not uncommon, that it was the illness that made their father behave this way. They understood that one person can be singled out as a scapegoat and receive all of the sufferer's frustration. In his better moments, Leslie's brother was able to understand and accept this, even feel honored that his father felt safe enough with him to let all this emotion go, but to be the recipient of all this anger was taking a toll on the younger man. How does one receive all this from one's own father and not respond in anger too? How does one receive but not absorb all this negativity? He didn't want to step away from the care he was giving to his father and especially to his mother, but dealing with it all was a great challenge.

Leslie explained to me that, although her father's behavior was exacerbated by his dementia, in fact, it was not uncharacteristic of him. He had always been a deeply unhappy man. Now, in his old age, he no longer had a way of distracting himself from the unhappiness that had plagued him all his life and had nothing to look forward to that would relieve it. Although he had his wife of many years still by his side, although he had his successful and caring children there to attend to him, although he had plenty of money and the best medical care, in his mind, he had nothing.

As his mind deteriorated, he seemed less and less able to understand what was happening around him, but he had a surprising ability to focus on one or two themes. One major theme for him was money: He was sure he didn't have enough of it. He called me regularly to ask about his account. I, of course, never saw the anger that Leslie had described to me. Despite his dementia, he was able to control his feelings outside the family. I did see, however, how terribly confused he had become, how it was impossible to talk to him because he would repeatedly come back to the same question of how broke he was. Over and over I would review the numbers with him, and he would be appeased. But the next day he would call once again with the same questions. We would go over the numbers again. Finally, it got to the point where he would not be appeased, where he no longer believed me when I told him how much money he had. He was sure he was one step away from the poorhouse. He would forget what I had said about the balance in his account before we got to the end of the conversation. Eventually, he no longer even understood the numbers I gave him, and we could no longer converse.

> There are only two emotions, love and fear, and for this poor man, only fear remained.

To my mind the saddest part of this situation was his anxiety. He had plenty of money for whatever he needed, and his family was being very prudent in managing it, but the anxiety he felt, his feeling of being poor and desperate, was painful to witness and, I'm sure, even more painful to experience. No facts could relieve his anxiety. He was left only with the fear, and it was in part this fear that spawned his anger.

Just as he could no longer believe he had money, he also could not believe he had love. He became suspicious of his family and felt he could not trust them. He began to believe they were plotting against him. He regularly chastised his family members, especially this one son who had been singled out to receive the worst. He lashed out every day with angry words and accusations. His family had to deal more and more with his unreasonable anger. And, of course, as they listened to this ugliness, they had to deal with their own strong reactions.

Obviously some of the behavior that this man displayed was part and parcel of his disease. Alzheimer's and dementia patients often display anger and suspicion and often single out one person as their main target. I am not equipped to evaluate how much of this unhappy man's behavior grew out of the disease and how much had been brewing all his life, but unfortunately neither was his family. They wanted to believe that all of this was only the result of his disease, but his lifetime unhappiness made it easy to imagine that some of it had been simmering deep within him forever. Their own responses ranged from understanding one day to anger the next, from despair one moment to hurt and confusion the next. Anger is anger, and to have to deal with it each day, to listen to it, and to respond maturely is a very difficult task. As Leslie said to me, "I can say that it is only the disease talking, but it still cuts deep and still makes my blood boil." She told me with great sadness in her voice that one day, she had tried to reason with him, tried to point out to him that he had so much more than others and that he didn't seem grateful for anything he had. She had pointed to all the love that was around him, his sound financial situation, and his relative good health. He looked her straight in the eye and said, "None of that matters to me."

Eventually, this man became almost completely incapacitated. Much of the burden of caring for him physically was removed when he entered a nursing home but not the emotional burden. He remained bitter and angry, complained every day, refused to eat. All the members of the family had to find a way to deal with the man's anger as well as their own. They all had to find a constructive way to channel the emotion that their father's condition stirred up. And all of them had to find a way of maintaining contact with the man who was their father as he progressed sadly toward his death. They had to deal not only with the sadness of his decline but also with the sadness at the way this decline was taking place. It was far from what we all imagine to be "dying of old age." It was harsh, painful, and filled with challenge.

For Leslie, handling and caring for the family's investment portfolio became a constructive way of honoring her father and also contributing to his care. He had, after all, taught her much of what she knew about investing. He had loved investing and she did too. To oversee this portfolio deliberately and consciously was something she could do and do well. It became her official responsibility as well as her path to greater insight. She did it lovingly in order to relieve her mother of this task and also to honor what was positive in her relationship with her father.

Money is the bridge between our values and our material world.

When we would talk to consider some aspect of this sizable portfolio, she always generously shared her thoughts not only on old age but also on anger. For Leslie, anger was the theme of old age. In her family, her father's old age and his illness became the opportunity that the universe presented to her to examine, understand, and transcend anger. The beautiful story that I saw unfold was the story of how Leslie, a remarkable woman, turned her own anger into compassion and used her relationship to money as the tool.

Over the months leading up to her father's death, Leslie described the stages she herself went through in dealing with her strong emotions vis-à-vis her father. How at first, she blamed him, believing that he could act differently but that he was choosing to act in the way that he did. At that stage, she had tried to talk him out of his anger and convince him that he had no right and certainly no reason to be so angry. When this failed, she had become angry herself. What felt like his recalcitrance brought out a deep anger in her. She wanted to kick him for the way it had kept him from loving her. She still wanted him to be the father and to be in charge. She was still looking for the relationship that she had somehow imagined as a child. Here she was offering him love and looking for him to love her in return. Instead, he was demanding something she couldn't provide.

Leslie understood that to blame her father would get her nowhere. She knew that to blame him only kept her feeling like a victim and a child. Courageous as she was, she was not afraid to look at this anger and how it had infected her entire family, how she herself had married a very angry and unhappy man, who, like her father, kept himself at a distance most of the time. Although she was no longer married to this man, she understood that this failed marriage was part of the legacy of anger in her family. And although she didn't have to deal too much with her ex-husband anymore, her children did. The legacy of anger and unhappiness had thus touched yet another generation. "How many generations have carried this anger?" she wondered aloud one day. "Surely it didn't originate with my father." As she thought back to what she knew of earlier generations, she realized that her father was, in fact, just one more in a long line of anger's victims.

Anger was the theme that informed not only her father's old age but also the life of her whole family. Some of her brothers and sisters seemed to be stuck in it, too, just as her father was. One brother in particular seemed to have internalized this family pattern of behavior, getting angry at every sharp remark from his father while remaining oblivious to the sharp remarks he himself directed at others. He defended himself against the anger of others by meeting it with his own. Another family member became upset each time the group needed to consider some new decision that had to be made regarding their father's care. If the family did not agree with her point of view, she became quite anxious. She was unable or unwilling to sit back and let events take their course. She was in a great hurry to resolve things, perhaps because taking action was easier than allowing difficult emotions to come to the surface. Part of her defense against her father's decline was to control and to arrange. Activity kept her from having to accept uncertainty and the difficulty of their situation.

> Money is the mirror in which we glimpse our true selves.

For some of the family members, talk of their father's disease as the cause of his anger was very unwelcome. They preferred to see his mean-spirited behavior as the essential man; to view him this way gave them permission to respond in a mean-spirited way themselves. To accept that some of his behavior was surely the result of his illness would have called upon them to act compassionately toward a person who was not at all pleasant to deal with. It was easier for them to be angry than to be compassionate. They preferred to behave in the same old way rather than consider a more mature response. To be loving toward those who love us back is easy. To show compassion toward those who are cruel and hurtful is infinitely more challenging.

But for Leslie it was different; compassion was what she sought in her life and what she hoped to achieve. She intuitively understood that to be compassionate in this very difficult situation would be her greatest challenge and her richest reward. If she could transcend her anger here, where family ties brought emotions so close to the surface, she could truly grow. If she could feel compassion here, she could feel it anywhere. And so each time she felt angry, she stopped to reflect. Each time she felt her anger begin to creep into her mind, she tried to defuse it. Of course, it gradually lost its hold on her. Eventually, she felt less angry less often, and when her anger did arise, she was able to control it. Anger at her unhappy father was replaced by disappointment and a sense of sadness that he couldn't have enjoyed his life more. She told me how she had reviewed her childhood and thought sadly about how little time she had enjoyed with him. She was able to conjure up only three happy memories of time spent with her father when she had felt his love and his full attention. But now, rather than blame him, she felt a strong resolve to break this cycle with her own children. And because she still felt love for her elderly father, she held fast to those three good memories.

Leslie's "Spread-the-Joy" relationship to her money eased the pain of her father's decline.

Leslie had come to understand another important feature of dealing with her father. She had come to appreciate that the essence of their connection now, as everything was reduced to the bare essentials, was about connection alone. Their interactions were not about the content of their words; they were about connecting, communicating, being in each other's presence. If they had the same conversation over and over, what did it matter? What was important was that they were having a conversation. She, in the "prime" of her life, could reflect upon the future and the past of their relationship. But he, in a phase of his life perhaps far more important than what we call the "prime," a phase that may be worth all the rest, a phase where all is reduced to the essential, could reflect upon their words only in the here and now. And the here and now was all that mattered. With all financial worries set aside, there remained for Leslie only the essential issue of communication. What they spoke of was unimportant; that they connected with each other was all that counted.

Leslie related to me a story of a good visit with her father in the nursing home. She had promised to come early to share a cup of morning coffee. Being especially lucid that day, he asked if they could review his accounts. So they sat together as they had so many times before and went over each stock and bond position and the performance of the entire account. He seemed quite pleased with the discussion but then, five minutes later, asked if they could review the accounts. They began again, reviewing each stock and bond position and the performance of the account in general. Once again, he was quite pleased and once again, after five minutes, asked to review the accounts. Within an hour, they went over things four times, each time with the same interest and freshness as the first. Finally it was time for Leslie to leave. He asked to accompany her to the elevator. Slowly they made their way, he leaning on a walker, she holding his arm. When they arrived at the elevator, he drew himself up to his full height, a most professional and businesslike expression on his face. "Thank you so much for coming by," he said with a smile, "and when my daughter arrives, we will go over these accounts together."

It would be easy to see this story as sad, but Leslie's interpretation was different. They had had a good conversation, most satisfying to both. They had connected and talked and enjoyed each other. She was able to feel love for him. He, although it finally appeared that he did not recognize his daughter, was able to express his appreciation of her. When all that was peripheral was stripped away, there remained for them only the essential: They had connected. And like so many times before, they had connected over money! Would that all conversation was made of this.

The Elderly Person's Financial Issues

Leslie's story isn't about the complications of making an investment portfolio work for an elderly person, but it does underscore how vulnerable an elderly person can be and how emotionally complicated it can be to accept the responsibility for caring for that person. I believe that in this situation, it's imperative to understand our own emotional state as we begin to handle another family member's money. There is simply too much room for emotions to get the better of us, and money provides too easy a mechanism for acting out those emotions if we're not self-aware.

In addition to all the emotional, medical, and practical issues that there are to deal with as people age, there are also some significant financial ones. I'm referring here primarily to the day-to-day management of an older person's money. Although this task may seem daunting, in fact, the choices are fairly simple. Unlike the other life situations discussed in *The Value of Money*, in this one, the financial issues can be viewed from one perspective alone. The number-one priority, and often the only goal, is to provide care for an elderly person for the rest of his or her life.

When we plan a portfolio for a younger person, we're almost always considering multiple goals and differing points of view. Retirement planning, for example, often includes other simultaneous goals like providing for the education of children or generating growth as well as income. But in the financial care of an elderly person, there are usually only two priorities: to provide enough income to buy the care that's needed and, especially if the investment portfolio is not sizable, to make money last as long as possible.

It is true that sometimes we also plan a bit for the heirs of elderly family members. Sometimes, if there's plenty of money and it's clear that the older people won't outlive their resources, a portion of the portfolio can be structured to provide for the heirs. But doing so can seem inappropriate to the younger people taking charge of the financial duties. They're often the heirs themselves and handling money with themselves in mind can seem selfish or greedy. Thus the focus of most caretakers usually remains squarely on the needs of the elderly. That means that the focus is on people with whom they have had a very long and most often complicated history.

One of the great challenges of caring for an elderly family member's money is remaining detached on the one hand and compassionate on the other. A sort of "loving detachment" can be very helpful in this situation. Cool detachment guided by love and concern makes for the most reasoned and best decisions. It sounds simple, of course, but oh what a tall order it is!

Those who are able to take over with love and compassion are wonderful to observe. They make every decision with only the older person in mind. They weigh every action with compassion and concern for their parents' dignity, comfort, safety, and care. I suspect these are families with a long history of love and respect. Caring for their parents in a loving way would be the only choice these people could contemplate. It's easy to love a loving person, and handling another's money in this way can be a great act of love.

There are others, however, for whom this job takes on a very different color. I have, on occasion, seen individuals use this situation as one more opportunity to dredge up every mean-spirited thing a parent has ever done. Every financial decision that has to be made or every action that needs to be taken is seen as just one more imposition by a demanding parent. The irony of this, of course, is that while the parent may have been very mean over the years, the child is doing no better. I remember one man who complained bitterly of his mother's lifetime selfishness. He resented terribly having to handle her affairs as she got older. Even as he regularly called her a selfish woman, he helped himself to an inordinately large "salary" from her estate for the duties he was performing. While it's not illegal to pay oneself for serving as a trustee for another family member, his pay was generous indeed. "I deserve it!" he claimed.

What we give the world is given to us. Selfishness begets selfishness.

While it's easy to love a loving person and, I suppose, easy to justify selfish behavior toward a selfish person, it's those who match a parent's anger or selfishness with love who are the most impressive. That was certainly the case for Leslie, who used her money responsibilities to grow and develop. I have seen few people approach this task with her degree of awareness and deliberation.

Still, I have to say that, although I've seen some nasty stories over the years, I've seen more inspiring ones. We may be hesitant to accept this responsibility, we may regret it terribly, but most of us do it with a measure of grace. We rise to the occasion. This task of taking over the care of an elderly parent is filled with opportunity for kindness, and money is just one part of it.

It seems to me that managing our parents' money on their behalf is more difficult emotionally than it is intellectually. The financial issues are fairly straightforward while the emotional ones are more complex. Being called upon to make significant decisions for our parents as they become more vulnerable can hardly be a joyous task. The emotions it can bring up—sadness, regret, fear, greed—are all compounded by the very real physical demands of caring for an elderly person who isn't likely to improve much. We all know that the inevitable end to this journey is death.

But at the same time, this is one of life's great opportunities to give selflessly. To my mind, it's a sacred duty to a person who deserves our care, who cared for us, and who is at a needy stage of life. If for no other reason than the fact that most of us will reach that stage of life ourselves and might benefit from contemplating it, this period of life deserves our attention. No matter how much history has preceded this endeavor, it's still an opportunity to be conscious, aware, caring, and responsible.

How to Begin

So where do you start as you take over for your aging parents or as you allow your children to begin to assume responsibility for your money? Once again, there is a "best-of-all-possible-worlds" scenario.

If ever there was a time for honest conversation, this is it. This is the time for parent and child to lay it all out on the line. And I'm not speaking only of financial matters but also of the emotional issues behind them. How much easier would this stage of life be for both generations if children knew exactly what parents wanted and parents could have a say in the decisions made on their behalf? From the point of view of the younger generation, wouldn't we like to know how our parents are really feeling as they enter this phase of their life? And wouldn't we as the older generation like to think that we have had some control over what happens to us as we age?

Often I think we avoid asking our parents what their greatest fears are, their fondest hopes; it isn't easy to talk about decline and death in this way. Are they more concerned with staying in their home if possible or with living near one of their children? Is their personal safety an issue or rather proximity to medical professionals? How do they feel about their money? Are they afraid of running out, or are there some special things they would like to see happen to it? Many people, for example, like to make sure that the gifts they have been giving to charities or to family members are continued. Sometimes people have commitments, like a pledge to a church, for example, a semester's tuition for a grandchild, or a special gift to a friend. They will want to be sure these obligations are fulfilled, and that may become our job.

This time need not be depressing, however. Getting to know your parents from the point of view of their money can be an interesting opportunity to understand your own relationship to yours. First of all, if you've never talked about this with them, it might be very interesting to learn some of their money stories. How did they earn it? What were the high points in their investing history? And what were their low points? Investment portfolios have stories too, and sometimes they're fascinating. It's possible you'll see a very different side of your parents as they talk about their money.

My own family is a good case in point. I only came to appreciate how much my father enjoyed working with money and numbers when I began helping him with his investments. And only after he had passed away and I began to work with my mother on this same portfolio did I realize that her attitude toward risk was somewhat different from his. Both of these things have made me understand my own relationship to my money far better than I did before.

From the point of view of the parent, this stage of letting go of some control can be challenging. Over the years I have seen many people accept the help of their children gracefully, but others do not find it so easy to do, even though it may come as a relief. Relinquishing control of something as central to our day-to-day lives as our money is understandably a challenge. It's not surprising that it is, for some, an unwelcome change.

I've seen many families play a sort of "What-if?" game in order to ease into conversations about this situation. "What if you can no longer drive, what would you like us to do?" "What if you can't really live in your house anymore because of the stairs, what type of place might you enjoy?" "What if you feel isolated where you are now, where would you like to go?" Talking about possible scenarios can go a long way toward creating an atmosphere of trust and understanding. It permits both parties—or more, if appropriate—to talk about the options and the realities. It might make later decisions far easier and relieve some of the uncertainty around them.

As this kind of discussion unfolds, all parties can turn their attention to the money itself. Fortunately, there are some concrete steps to follow to get a handle on a parent's financial life.

Getting a Handle on the Money

The first step is to *take an inventory*. It's important to know exactly what financial resources a person has and what form they're in. Are there multiple bank or brokerage accounts? It's important to check around to see if everything has been accounted for. Many people, not only the elderly, have rather scattered financial lives.

Step 2 is to *check the form these assets are in.* I'm referring here to the title on the accounts. Are assets held jointly between husband and wife or does each person have his or her own accounts? Is there a trust or maybe a couple of trusts? If so, have all financial assets (investments, bank accounts, etc.) been put into the name of the trust? Has your parents' home been put into the trust? Their car? It's not at all uncommon to discover, long after a trust is established, that there are still a few items that haven't made their way into the name of the trust. If one parent has already passed away, has that person's name been removed from all accounts? Are there other types of accounts like, for example, a charitable remainder trust or a life insurance trust?

Step 3 involves *your right to act on your parents' behalf.* Once you're familiar with all the assets that there are and know that they're in the proper form, it's important to be sure that you, as caretaker, can act for them at all the financial institutions involved. This will mean that you must have some form of power of attorney. Some institutions make a distinction between a full authorization to act on behalf of your parent and a limited one. (The difference usually involves your right to withdraw money from the account or not.) Although most institutions will accept a legally drawn-up power of attorney, most will also require that you and your parent sign one of their own forms. Your legal adviser can help you with all these details. But it's key to realize here that your parent must be able to sign this authorization. Waiting until they're no longer able to do this will make the whole process extremely difficult.

Step 4 is another type of inventory, *an inventory of people.* Who are the professionals with whom your parents have been dealing, especially in their recent years? If you don't already know them, you should meet your parents' financial adviser, banker, lawyer, and CPA. If these people have worked closely with your parents over the years, they know a great deal about your family's financial life and history. They may, in fact, know more about it than you do if they have had a close working relationship with your parents. And if you're working with a situation where your parents can no longer discuss things with you because of illness, these professionals may have many clues as to your parents' wishes. Financial advisers, for example, spend almost as much time talking about hopes, dreams, and emotions as they do about money.

Step 5 may seem a little surprising as you're in the midst of taking over the care of your parents and trying to figure out so many things at once. But as you're reviewing all that pertains to your parents' financial life, it's also good to look beyond their life to see if there is a *will* or *trust* in place to offer direction for the distribution of their estate after death. Nothing brings out rivalries and problems in a family like money. A well-thought-out will or trust can solve problems before they arise.

Of course, writing a will or establishing a trust are things you can't do for your parents. They must make the decisions that constitute an estate plan, and they must execute the legal documents. But you can gently prod them in that direction if they haven't already done so or encourage them to review their wills and trusts if it has been some time since they were executed. Although this may seem a bit inappropriate or uncomfortable, it's a great service to all the members of your family, including your parents. Most people find that they feel quite peaceful and pleased when these kinds of plans are in order.

All of these things—the discussions, the inventories, and the estate-plan review—are still not getting down to the nitty-gritty of managing your parents' money. That brings us to Step 6, the issues and challenges that must be considered as you begin to actually *make decisions on their investments.*

Obviously one of the prime concerns relating to their money will be safety. In truth, there is a measure of risk in every investment, even the most conservative, but there are some investments that are inappropriate for an older person in most cases. Obviously these are the investments with a greater risk of loss. Although these may have tremendous potential for gain, they also have significant potential for loss. That's not to say that everything in an older person's portfolio should carry some sort of guarantee or should be ultraconservative. A great deal depends upon how much money is available for investment, how much income a portfolio needs to generate, and how it is already invested.

When sitting down with a client in this situation, I like to begin with the question of income. How much income is needed to cover your parents' expenses? What are the existing sources of income? When we see what the gap is between what's needed and what's coming in from various sources (social security, pensions, other types of retirement plans, etc.), we can easily set goals for what the investment portfolio needs to furnish.

Let's say for example that a person's expenses are roughly $4,000 per month or $48,000 per year. If retirement plans plus social security provide approximately $30,000, then our short-fall is $18,000. Now let's assume our parents' investment portfolio equals $350,000. To generate $18,000 with a portfolio of $350,000 our goal would be to earn roughly 5.1 percent. Assuming that the prevailing interest rates on high-quality bonds are at that level at the time, we could generate the needed $18,000. But it would require that almost all of that $350,000 be committed to high-grade bonds with no money left over for other types of investment.

But let's assume that the portfolio is twice that, or $700,000. Now there can be more flexibility. There's easily enough money to generate the needed $18,000 per year in income and still allocate some money in investments that offer less income but more growth potential (blue chip stocks for example.) This obviously affords greater diversification, and is a more desirable situation. A little bit of growth, even in the most conservative portfolio, offers a potential safety net in the case of either very long life or greater need as time goes by.

But what if your situation is the opposite? What if your parents' portfolio is not large enough to generate the interest needed to close the gap between income being received and income needed? Let's say, for example, your parents' investment portfolio equals $200,000. In order to generate the needed $18,000, it would have to earn 9 percent per year, a rather high interest rate in most circumstances. You and your parents would face the very real possibility of having to dig into that principal of $200,000 in order to provide what's needed. Potentially the money can still be invested to earn interest at whatever is the prevailing rate for high-grade bonds, but, above and beyond that, you will be using some of that original $200,000.

For many people, that's a scary proposition. They see the value of their nest egg going down slowly, and of course that doesn't feel good. They calculate how long the money can last and worry that it will run out before their parents' death. Some older people regret that they may not in fact be able to leave anything to their kids. But sometimes this is the reality. Although saving to have money at the end of our life isn't nearly as exciting as saving for retirement or a great vacation, nonetheless, this too is what our money is for. I have often said to people who worry about the high expenses of care for the elderly, "If your money is not for this, then what on earth is it for?!"

In some circumstances, revamping a portfolio may generate more income or provide more security. Just as safety needs to be a primary focus in an elderly person's portfolio, so too does flexibility. As we all know, the situation of an elderly person can change dramatically and very quickly. One fall, one small stroke can change everything for an older person. Your parent, who has been living independently, can suddenly need care, a new living situation, medical attention. And as your parents' physical or mental situation changes, so does their financial picture. It's very important that their money be set up in ways that permit change as needed. From an investment point of view, this means that there must be liquidity in the portfolio. Everyone's situation is different of course, but generally speaking there must be assets that can be sold easily and without undue penalty in order to generate cash. While there certainly can be some longer-term investments in an older person's portfolio, there also need to be some shorter-term ones. These provide greater flexibility for the simple reason that they will mature or redeem soon. The stocks that are held should be ones that trade actively, so that, should you need to sell them, there will be no difficulty finding a buyer through the normal channels of stock trading. And in case of emergency there should be cash that can be accessed without having to sell anything. This can be in very short-term CDs, money-market funds, or savings accounts.

Keeping It Simple

When we design a portfolio in other circumstances, we spend a lot of time thinking about such issues as the asset allocation (how much stock versus how much bond to meet a person's needs), risk tolerance (how aggressive can you be in order to achieve the goal but also maintain your comfort), time horizon (how long do you have to achieve your goals), the need for income (are you currently using any of the money to live on), and the need for growth (what return would you like to achieve in order to arrive at your long-term goal). In the case of an elderly person, however, all are often rather straightforward.

Asset allocation is often directly affected by how much income the investor wishes to generate. Risk tolerance is very often low unless the portfolio is very large. The time horizon is, unfortunately, often rather short. Unlike retirement planning, for example, where we might have twenty years to go before income will be needed, here income is needed right now. Although it may also be needed for several years to come as our entire population is living longer and longer, still we're almost always dealing with present as opposed to future need, and income is almost always an important goal for the elderly.

An older person's portfolio can be a fairly simple one and often has already been set up in an appropriate fashion. Accepting the role of financial caretaker may be only a matter of assuming the supervision of a portfolio of investments that is already up and running. The only challenge then is to remain very focused on a parent's needs and to evaluate everything in that light. The financial part of a job like this is easy, but the emotional part can be tricky.

As we take over the money duties for an elderly parent, it's easy to feel like an intruder, especially in a family that doesn't talk openly about money. It's not uncommon for a financial caretaker to feel concern about what brothers and sisters are thinking, concern that they might feel you are managing things in a way that favors yourself over them. People often worry that they're making a decision that the parent would not approve of, especially if that parent has been an active investor. There's the inevitable and very real fear of disappointing or messing up. In my experience, most financial caretakers are very respectful and careful as they take on this responsibility.

Managing the financial life of an elderly parent is a wonderful service and a great gift to offer a loved one. It's an act of love to honor a parent's wishes and care for his or her money. If done responsibly, it's also a great service to the rest of the family. An extra set of eyes on an older person's money can be very important. Unfortunately, in our society, the elderly too often fall prey to scam artists. Managing the money of elderly parents' responsibly protects them from those who would take advantage of them. Working with your parents and with their trusted advisers is a way to shield them from harm.

As our parents age and approach the last stages of life, there are so many concerns for family members that can be far more significant than money. With the financial situation under control, the entire family can focus with love and respect on the physical and emotional needs of a parent. Getting the financial house in order may seem dry and dull, especially in the turmoil of caring for an elderly family member, but it's a valuable service to offer. It provides comfort and care. It may go a long way toward quelling potential family disputes. A well-ordered financial situation frees up the whole family to focus on life and death instead of on money. I dare say it frees us up to focus on something far more important than money— love.

7.

LOSS OF A LOVED ONE

When I began my work as a financial adviser, I had no idea how often I would deal with death. It simply hadn't occurred to me that I'd be asked to confront death on such a regular basis. Although most of what we do is manage money around our clients' lives, we also spend quite a bit of time considering it in relation to their deaths.

The death of a person with money raises all kinds of important financial issues. Most aspects of estate planning, if not all of them, are an attempt to plan what's to happen to our money after we die: Who is to receive what? In what form is the money to pass to heirs? At what age are beneficiaries to receive their money? How are taxes to be paid? The list of financial questions that come up in conjunction with death goes on and on, but these complications, issues, and concerns are nothing compared to those that are raised by one particular death—that of a spouse.

I believe that the death of a spouse is one of the most stressful events in the life of any adult. Grief, sorrow, anger, and fear all combine to burden a surviving spouse for months and sometimes years, and the money concerns that such a death can cause often compound that burden. Financial matters often draw grieving widows and widowers into a bureaucratic maze that can seem tedious and frustrating, and all at a time when they're least able emotionally, or least inclined intellectually, to think clearly and make decisions. To say the least, it's a situation filled with great potential for frustration, tension, and mistakes.

But it needn't be so. As with all the life events I discuss in *The Value of Money*, the death of a loved one too can present an opportunity to face our deepest fears about money and to resolve them. Despite all the challenge and all the pain, it can be a time of grace and growth.

I have experienced most of the life transitions that I discuss in *The Value of Money* personally. My reflections come from my observation of many clients as well as from my own life. But in speaking about this terrible loss, I must rely on my observation of the many people I've dealt with and on what they have told me. I'm very aware that there may be deep and hidden responses of which I'm unaware. I don't believe an experience as dramatic as the loss of a spouse can ever be truly understood until one has actually experienced it. Nonetheless, over the years I have worked with many people who have gone through this transition.

An Overwhelming Challenge

Few disruptions in our lives are as dramatic as the death of a spouse. For quite some time, everything stops. All other issues take a backseat as a family deals with all that such a death brings up. Eventually though, slowly I'm sure, some aspects of normal day-to-day life intrude and demand attention. One of these, inevitably, will be money.

The death of a spouse pushes the survivor into a major reevaluation of a complete financial picture. From income stream to spending patterns, from an investment plan to an estate plan, all aspects of an individual's finances must be reexamined. It may not mean that things will dramatically change, but occasionally it does. Sometimes a family's circumstances, and therefore its finances, change quite significantly after there's been such a death. One of the hardships of this reevaluation of a family's financial life is that the task must often be undertaken when people have very little appetite for it. I've seen this job overwhelm people. It can be discouraging, tedious, or downright frightening. But I've also seen people meet the challenge with dignity and courage.

Grief is a lonely business. Experts tell us that the average person grieves the death of a spouse for several years, and yet I've heard from clients that friends and relatives often expect a grieving wife or husband to "get over it" in a few weeks. At times, grief can turn very serious, resembling deep depression or post-traumatic stress syndrome. Dealing with mundane tasks, like those that finances present, can be most unwelcome. On the other hand, occasionally, individuals welcome these tasks as a diversion, something to do, a way to occupy the mind.

For many people thrust into the decision making that follows the death of a spouse, the financial world is unfamiliar territory. If the deceased person was the one who handled the money, the poor survivor may feel quite ill equipped to step into this new role. In fact, it can be the last thing one wishes to do. For many people with whom I've worked, the details involved in so many of the necessary decisions have seemed daunting and the bureaucratic requirements endless. At a time when they feel paralyzed by sorrow, the financial world asks them to perform a number of technical and unpleasant tasks related to their money. Add to that the pressure of well-meaning friends and family members whose suggestions can make things even worse.

For example, I've seen widows and widowers (in my experience, mostly widows) pressured to think about financial matters as early as the funeral itself. ("Did John have a life insurance policy? Have you contacted the insurance company? You know, my dear, you really must consider a trust.") Even when spoken out of the greatest concern for a grieving survivor, these types of comments following too soon after a spouse's death only add to the confusion. They make people feel that they should be doing things they don't really have the heart for yet. It causes them worry or it adds to their sadness, and the truth is that in most cases it isn't necessary to tackle financial matters right away. It's simply too much, and there's often little to gain.

In fact, there's danger in acting too quickly to address financial matters after the death of a spouse. In the midst of your grief, it's easy to make some basic, albeit understandable, mistakes. The problem is that sometimes these mistakes can have a very negative long-term impact. Allowing yourself time to grieve before taking on too many financial decisions is a good thing.

One financial mistake that I have seen clients make is to *rush into some major changes in their lives* simply to be doing something. Activity can certainly be a comfort in the middle of grief, but, from a financial point of view, too much change without the proper evaluation that should go with it can be costly.

Other people find themselves making reckless decisions with very little forethought, just to get it all over with. It's true that some of the financial work that must be done after a death might seem tedious and laborious. Nonetheless, the decisions to be made are important and should not be taken lightly.

Others, for whom financial decisions are a burden, make a different mistake: They *turn their financial futures over to someone else* in an effort to avoid it all together. This too is dangerous. Even when the person acting on your behalf has your best interests at heart, it's better to stay involved with your money. No one will ever care about it the way you do. Nor will anyone else have to live with any mistakes the way you will.

And finally there's another common error that isn't nearly as dangerous but is nonetheless regrettable. Many a grieving widow or widower has *taken out their anger and sorrow* on the poor functionaries who work at the banks, insurance companies, brokerage firms, or human resources departments with which they must speak in order to claim their benefits. Employee benefits, for example, can be quite complicated and the terminology often unfamiliar. As much as the benefits representatives want to help and as much as they deal with this situation every day as part of their jobs, they cannot, of course, share your grief. Anger, frustration, and impatience are understandable, but they certainly don't help. In the middle of your grief, it's easy to forget that these employees are just trying to do their job. In the middle of their day-to-day work, it's easy for them to forget your grief.

All of these reactions are understandable, but they are compounded if you are someone with an unfortunate or uncomfortable relationship to money. A bit of planning, however, along with a good measure of patience and courage, can help you avoid mistakes and move gracefully into the new phase of life that the death of a spouse inevitably represents.

Achieving a Balance

One thing is certain: The death of a loved one is a very emotional event. No one expects it to be any different. But allowing grief, sorrow, anger, and fear to dictate your financial decisions is dangerous. Whether you experience paralysis or frustration or crushing sorrow, the great challenge is to understand what part your emotions are playing in your thinking and to allow yourself time to get through this stressful period with grace. This is not to say that your emotions shouldn't play a role in your decision making; they should and they must. This is to say that your decisions need not be solely dictated by your strong emotions. Many are able to achieve this balance and more.

One of the most extraordinary clients I have ever worked with was a woman who displayed such grace in just this situation. She was also a person who made her financial decisions with a kind of raw courage not often seen in the financial world. In fact this woman's whole life seemed to be about courage.

Cheryl was referred to me by a friend from her church who had been my client for some time, and I liked her the minute we began to talk. She phoned, asking to schedule an appointment to review her situation. I always like to get as much information as possible before an appointment, and so we took a moment to speak right then. She told me what she felt she needed her money to accomplish and how much money she was dealing with. She had a firm and pleasant voice and was very articulate in discussing her circumstances. She was also considerate of my time, which I appreciated. It seemed to me that she would be an easy and very pleasant person to deal with.

We arranged a time to meet, and then, almost as an afterthought, she asked if our office was wheelchair accessible. This surprised and interested me. We had spoken at some length and about some fairly personal things, but not until the very end of our conversation did she mention that she was in a wheelchair and then almost in passing. Perhaps she had found, over the years, that once people knew about the wheelchair, they focused too much on it. Or perhaps her disability was the least important part of her identity in her own mind, at least as it pertained to our work together. Whatever it was, I was intrigued.

When I finally met Cheryl, I was immediately struck by a kind of visual oxymoron. Here was a tiny woman whose body was crippled and slightly twisted. Her torso didn't seem to be made up of many parts but, rather, of one almost solid one. Of course I knew how ridiculous that idea was, but still that was my initial thought. In contrast to that, however, almost as if it belonged on a different body, was her face: bright, intelligent, and very animated! Cheryl presented herself with every bit as much energy as everyone else, but in her case, because of her disability, it was all concentrated in that vivid face. In our first meeting, I was struck by the way in which her facial expression held my attention.

Cheryl's husband accompanied her to that first appointment. He was a quiet man and didn't seem to be too involved in the discussion. Although the money was jointly owned, it really was she who seemed to be in charge of it. It was she who asked all the questions. And I imagined that it would be she who would be making the final decisions. However, there was really nothing too unusual about that. Often one member of a couple is the decision maker for both. Cheryl's husband, however, didn't seem bored or unappreciative in any way. He simply didn't participate in the discussion. I assumed that he was quietly listening and would discuss it all with her later.

What was a bit unusual, however, was how decisive Cheryl was on their behalf. She knew exactly what they needed and what they were seeking. She listened carefully to my explanations and asked intelligent and pointed questions. Behind that animated face was a very sharp mind. We quickly began to design and implement an investment strategy for them.

Not long after we began our investing, however, things took a dramatic turn. Cheryl called to tell me that her husband had been diagnosed with Alzheimer's. Thinking back on my first meeting with them, of how distant he was and how quiet, I realized that she must have known or at least suspected that this diagnosis was coming. Perhaps at an earlier time in their life together he would have been more involved in the discussion, and they would have shared the decision making. Perhaps some of her decisiveness was a response to his gradual mental deterioration. Although I feel certain that Cheryl had always been fairly decisive, perhaps some of her self-assurance had grown as his world had dwindled. As is always the case with caretakers of those with Alzheimer's or dementia, at a certain point I'm sure she had little choice but to take over the running of their household. Of course, I had no way of knowing what he had been like before the disease had whittled away at his true personality, but the clarity and decisiveness that she displayed were the first of many indications to come that

Cheryl was a master at adapting to the circumstances with which she was presented. Clearly this was not the first tough situation she had been handed in life, and it was not to be the last.

This new development changed my thinking about their financial situation somewhat. I knew that we would need to revise our strategy, and it was not going to be a simple change. Physically, caring for him wouldn't be easy for her, and financially there would be challenges. It was difficult to know what they were going to need down the road. Neither of them was very old. Would both of them need to draw on this portfolio? How long would she care for him? Would she herself need care in the future?

I'm paid to worry about people's money, and I immediately began to worry about theirs. This wasn't a huge portfolio, and if a considerable amount of money were needed to care for him now, would it deplete her resources for later? How would she manage as she aged if too much of their money was used up now? Would there be enough for her lifetime, given what she and I both knew could be long and expensive care for him? I pored over their portfolio, pushing and pulling, looking for ways to meet his immediate needs and also her longer-range ones. How many difficult decisions, I wondered, had this woman faced in her lifetime?

One day, quite by accident, I ran into them in a store. His demeanor and appearance had changed so dramatically that I was quite taken aback. As the disease had depleted his mind, it also had siphoned his entire body of its energy, direction, and strength. His gait was like a monotonous voice—plodding and steady—as he pushed her chair and stared vacantly out over her head. Once again, her animated face was such a contrast to his almost inert body that I couldn't help but be riveted by it.

To my great surprise, not long after that, Cheryl called to tell me that her husband had passed away. Of course, she was lonely without him and grieved his passing. She shed a few quiet tears as we spoke, but didn't seem comfortable displaying this emotion to me. She may have sought to downplay her disability in her dealings with others but certainly not her independence. In front of me, she was stoic, resigned, and graceful in her grief. And once again, we came together to rethink our investment strategy.

Cheryl recognized, as did I, an immediate and new financial challenge. Without her husband there in her home, she would have to make some changes in order to maintain the independence she so fiercely defended. She needed to set herself up in such a way that she could manage her day-to-day life from her wheelchair without the assistance of another person. She had already drawn on part of her portfolio to take good care of her husband. Now, more money would be needed for her to rearrange her living space. The same issue presented itself once again. If she withdrew more money now, would there be enough for later? But now the issues of love and responsibility that were part of caring for her husband were not determining factors. During his illness, I doubt that she even gave a passing thought to not offering him the best care they could afford, but now, it was love of herself that was the issue; it was her own life she was protecting. Sometimes caring for another is far easier than caring for oneself.

Cheryl made a courageous decision to withdraw more from her investments in order to build a specially equipped home, one that would allow her to remain alone. In addition, she had her car equipped with a device that pulled her wheelchair up once she was settled behind the wheel and stored it in a sort of luggage carrier.

I know that, on the face of it, the decisions Cheryl made may not seem too courageous. In a way, it seemed that she had little choice. If she wished to stay on her own, these were the things she needed to do. But I think that many people in her situation would have given up. Many would have been afraid to stay on their own. Many would have reasoned that no one would find fault with them if they chose an easier path and allowed themselves to become dependent. I believe most of us would have felt very sorry for ourselves in the same circumstances. Perhaps Cheryl allowed herself moments of feeling defeated or of wishing she could simply just give up. Perhaps she had moments when she doubted herself or her ability to do what she seemed so determined to do. But ultimately, she made her decisions quite matter-of-factly. We had several discussions about the financial side of things, and I'm sure that she had discussions with other advisers about other facets of these decisions. Then they were made, with simplicity and courage. She didn't seem to look back, to waiver, or to regret.

> Sometimes this is what an "All-Is-Well" attitude looks like—raw courage!

It seemed to me that Cheryl understood something we all give lip service to—living in the present. It wasn't that she had no regard for the future, but she had become a pro at dealing with what was. She told me once that one of the lessons her life had taught her was that "There's no guarantee tomorrow will be like today." And so Cheryl lived in and appreciated the present, did the best she could, and then moved forward. I doubt very much that she would have characterized her decision making as courageous at all; courage in the face of adversity had become just another good habit to her!

To me, however, her official financial worrier, her decisions seemed enormously courageous. My real fear was that she would outlive her money. Her choice was to live while she could. My fear was that, down the road, she would become dependent on others. She trusted her ability—and mine incidentally—to manage that portfolio so that she could maintain a quality life, even if it entailed compromises. She evaluated her life and her health, calculated how long she could remain independent, and then took a financial leap to make possible that independence in the here and now. She clearly understood that buying her independence now could be the very thing that would lead to her dependence later. She chose to live while she was alive. Never had I seen a person move through the death of a spouse with more grace and clarity. And rarely have I seen such a mature attitude toward money and its true role in a person's life. Cheryl truly did see money as her tool to use as she deemed most beneficial. She used it to achieve her goals of love as she cared for her husband and of independence and self-sufficiency as she cared for herself.

The Financial Issues Come in Stages

Given all the tension and the strong emotions that surround this unhappy life event, there's one piece of advice that most good advisers offer their clients right away: Do nothing. When you're dealing with this difficult situation, the best course of action may be to let some financial decisions wait for six months or so until you've grieved and become more clearheaded. If your financial situation is such that you don't have to rearrange things in order to meet your immediate needs, it's often better to do nothing immediately.

But sometimes, this slower course of action isn't possible. Sometimes decisions are thrust upon you because of your financial situation or because of the nature of the death. If death comes suddenly, and you have no time to prepare, there may be steps you need to take relatively quickly. Even then, however, some of the longer-range decisions can be put off until a calmer time.

The financial issues surrounding the death of a spouse come in stages. Fortunately, in most cases, there's very little that needs to be done immediately, and most families aren't too interested in thinking about money at the outset. The focus is generally on issues like arranging the funeral; communicating with family and friends; writing an obituary; keeping track of donations, flowers, and gifts; and dealing with all those who wish to express their love and concern. On top of having to cope with all the strong emotions that such a loss can provoke, these tasks are enough. As comforting as they are, they can also be exhausting.

There is, however, one small financial task that, if immediately performed, can be very helpful down the road, and it needn't be the surviving spouse who does so. If the deceased person owned stocks and bonds in a brokerage account, it can be very useful if *someone notifies the financial adviser* of the death right away, ideally on the day of death or the day after, so that your financial adviser can record the values of all securities on the exact date of death. Family members often need these figures later on. While advisers can certainly reconstruct these numbers later, it's much simpler to gather them if they record the numbers from that day or the day before. In my office, we simply print out a copy of the account statement for that day and keep it in the file for future reference. Having these values is especially important when the deceased person's assets are to be distributed not to a spouse but to other family members. These figures also may be needed in the valuation of the deceased person's estate, and they also establish the cost basis of all assets being passed to heirs.

But this detail is a small one compared to all of the others that must be dealt with when there has been a death. Sooner or later you will have to tackle bigger financial issues. Once you feel able to deal with business matters, it's time to evaluate your financial situation.

The Information-Gathering Phase

The first stage in this new evaluation of finances is quite mundane. It's the same first step that's involved in so many large transitions: *gathering information from a variety of sources.* The basic questions here are: "What financial assets did my deceased spouse own?" "Where and how are these assets held?" "What benefits am I entitled to as the surviving spouse?" "How do I go about claiming them?"

Professionals like your financial adviser and your lawyer can help you with some of this. They can certainly guide you through the conversations you will have with the variety of institutions you'll need to contact. As a practical matter, though, these organizations will require your permission to discuss your benefits or your accounts with any representative like a financial adviser or even a family member. They will need to be contacted by you directly.

Your goal at this phase of things is to contact several different organizations in order to understand what financial assets you are entitled to or responsible for, what procedures you must use to claim them, and what your options are for receiving money.

One of your first contacts will be the local social security office. In order to claim benefits or even discuss them with a social security representative, you'll need to present a death certificate, the social security number of the deceased person, and proof of your relationship (like a marriage certificate). Many people dread this task, but in fact it's quite important. At the death of your spouse, there may be benefits available to you as widow or widower, as well as to minor children who are still in school, that can be very important to your income. And although many people think of the government as a bureaucratic maze, my own experience in helping clients work with the Social Security Administration has been quite positive.

In addition to the social security people, you may need to contact the Office of Veteran's Affairs if your spouse was a veteran. They will be able to tell you if you're entitled to receive any benefits related to your spouse's service.

If your husband or wife owned life insurance and/or annuities, you must also contact the insurance companies involved. Many people find insurance issues rather complicated and the choices and paperwork confusing; it can be very helpful to have your financial adviser on the phone with you to ask questions and to interpret the answers you receive. The insurance company representatives will discuss the benefits you're entitled to, the choices you have as to how you'll receive the money, and the steps you must take to claim it. Although it isn't always necessary, it can be very helpful if you have the insurance policy itself that this representative will be referring to. Rarely do decisions have to be made right then and there. As in all of the tasks that must be performed after a death, there will be paperwork involved, and quite a bit of it. But that does give you time to think about what's best for you in your new life. And, here again, your financial adviser can be helpful as you fill out and process forms.

Of all the contacts you must make following the death of a spouse, one of the most important and in some ways the most complicated is the employee benefits department of your spouse's employer. There are a number of issues to take up with them, depending on whether your spouse was still working or had already retired. Again it can be very helpful to have a person like a trusted financial adviser who knows you and your financial situation on the line with you. There may be a variety of questions that arise as you speak. For example, you will be called upon to decide if you would like to take certain benefits in the form of a lump-sum distribution or in installments over your lifetime. You will need to decide how you wish to handle the taxation on these amounts. Over the years, I've done many a three-way call with clients and employers to discuss the variety of benefits that are often available.

The benefits you receive from your spouse's employer may well be your most important money as you go forward without him or her. For many people these benefits provide the most significant portion of their income. Not only may it be the largest sum you receive, but it may also be one of the more predictable portions of your income. Retirement monies that become available to you are often the largest single amount of money that you will ever have to work with in your life. Although it's certainly an unpleasant and difficult task to claim this money in the midst of all your grief, retirement money will be an important element, if not the corner-stone, of your financial future.

Understanding your benefits and the process through which you claim them is important. But how you take the money is equally important. If your spouse was still working, you're most likely the beneficiary on his or her 401(k) or 403(b) plan, pension, and/or employer-sponsored life insurance (including a supple-mental life insurance plan that many employees purchase). These are often pools of money that your spouse has been contributing to for years. They can be quite large and, when all of them are combined, can create a sort of windfall that must be dealt with. Some of the money [pension, 401(k), or 403(b)] may be eligible to be rolled over into an IRA to avoid any undue taxation. Other money, like life insurance, may be free and clear of taxes and so can be handled separately. A benefits representative, along with your financial adviser, can walk you through all of the available choices for receiving these monies.

In addition to all of the above, there's also health insurance to consider as well as other matters like long-term care insurance. Your spouse may have been contributing to these for some time. Once again, there will be quite a bit of paperwork to complete, but fortunately it isn't too complicated, and, in my experience at least, employee benefit representatives can be enormously helpful as you work your way through all the details of claiming your benefits.

Even if your spouse had already retired and was receiving some of his or her benefits, you still have to follow many of these same steps with an employer. In this situation, however, it may all be quite a bit simpler. For example, you and your spouse may have already begun receiving pension payments that will continue in full or in part, depending on how things were set up. Your spouse's 401(k) or 403(b) might have already been rolled over into an IRA. Nevertheless, a benefits representative can help you determine what steps you need to take to claim all the benefits to which you're entitled.

While you're in this information-gathering stage, there are other important contacts that you must make following a death. *Financial institutions* where your spouse held assets must also be notified. Brokerage accounts, joint checking accounts, savings accounts all need to be renamed. It's an unhappy task to take your deceased spouse's name off of these accounts, but eventually it must be done. You must also remember to notify any other type of financial institution where there may be an investment. It's not uncommon, for example, for people to own an investment that's not held with their others in a brokerage account but directly with the investment company. This can also be true of an annuity held through an insurance company and not reflected on a brokerage account statement. It's easy to miss these separately held investments. If assets remain in your deceased spouse's name, that can certainly be corrected later on, but, as years pass, this task becomes more and more complicated. It's best to handle everything at this time if possible.

If you and your spouse were cotrustees on a trust, you will need to remove your deceased spouse's name. You can then continue as sole trustee, or a successor trustee can assume the duty of cotrustee that your spouse held. Your trust document itself will spell out what your choices are in this instance and who is named to succeed the deceased person as trustee. You may want to visit with a qualified estate attorney who can help you with these details.

Once all of the information gathering is complete and the

mundane tasks are taken care of, you can begin the next phase of the financial overhaul that takes place after a death. This next stage of your work will be far less detail oriented and certainly less bureaucratic. Now, at last, it's time to step back and examine what you need and what you have.

The Income-Evaluation Phase

When I work with clients following the death of a spouse, I like to begin this evaluation phase with the *question of income*, often the most pressing issue. Hopefully your spouse's death has not caused a reduction in your income that forces you to make drastic changes. Ideally no adjustments are required. But sometimes there are changes, perhaps because your spouse was working and you've now lost that income or because a pension payment has been reduced. In any case, the questions to ask regarding income are fairly specific:

- What will be my sources of income?
- How much will I be receiving from each?
- Are there new sources of income (as in income from retirement benefits rolled into an IRA or from insurance proceeds)?
- How much can these new sources of income reasonably provide?
- How much income do I need to live on now as a single person?
- Is there a shortfall between what I will have coming in and what I need? a surplus?

Hopefully, this evaluation is a happy one, and no changes will be necessary. If, however, you don't have enough money coming in, adjustments may need to be made in your lifestyle. Do you need to consider less expensive housing? If you're still working, is there a better-paying job available? If you're no longer in the job force, do you need to consider going back to work or supplementing your income with some part-time work? These are the types of compromises that some people must consider.

On the other hand, it's often the case that a widow or widower finds the opposite situation. Sometimes there's more, not less, money to say grace over. When there's been a death, assets tend to get more consolidated because so many things pay out to the survivor. While this situation is certainly preferable, it too can present a burdensome responsibility.

If you find yourself the caretaker of a pot of money, you must design a strategy or investment plan, implement it, and begin the process of monitoring your portfolio. Depending on where you are in this grieving process, you may or may not be ready to take on all of that responsibility right away. In fact, once you know that your income needs will be met, you've moved the various pools of money into the proper accounts (retirement distributions into an IRA for example), and you've gone through all the paperwork of getting the correct titles on things, there's nothing wrong with letting the money sit quietly until you feel ready. Hopefully you won't need to let it sit idle for too long. Money must be invested to really work for you, but if your grief still weighs too heavy, overseeing an investment portfolio might just be more than you care to take on. In that case, give yourself a few more months.

The Portfolio-Construction Phase

Phase three of your work begins when you're ready to dig into your financial situation. At this point, it's wise to work with your financial adviser to evaluate more than just your income. This stage involves evaluating your entire financial situation and *constructing the investment portfolio* that will enable you to move forward. Once again there are some questions to ask:

- Do I understand what I own and the role each investment plays in my portfolio?
- Do the investments that I already owned with my spouse fit my temperament and needs as a single person? In other words, do I need to be more conservative with my money than we were as a couple? more aggressive?
- Is my portfolio, as it stands now, well balanced between stocks and bonds? If not, what do I need to add or to remove?
- Am I sufficiently diversified?
- Where should the cash that I have received from retirement plans or insurance be invested? This, of course, will depend on the answers given to all the previous questions.
- Do I need to consult with my attorney in order to review the estate plan that my spouse and I established together? Are there priorities I'd like to change or things I'd like to add? Do documents such as wills and trusts and/or beneficiary forms for IRAs, life insurance, annuities, or retirement plans need to be updated?

These issues are some of the basic elements of sound financial planning. A good adviser can walk you through this process and help you sort through your many choices.

Moving Toward Healing

Going on without your spouse is painful to be sure. In the midst of your grief, putting your financial house in order may seem tedious and mundane at best and crass and improper at worst. To some, it feels like an insurmountable task; to others, it's the means to the end they seek, a stepping-stone to healing. At the very least, an organized financial life and relief from money concerns will bring freedom to do the other things in your life that are important.

This was certainly the case with one client I was fortunate enough to work with. Her situation wasn't a happy one, but throughout she was clear about what she needed and wanted.

Janet was only in her fifties when, Tom, her husband of many years, passed away. I had worked with the family for some time, and so, when she was ready, Janet and her children came in to review her situation. We talked, as would be expected, about her late husband, about how her life had changed, her new priorities, and what she wished to do now.

The more we spoke the more concerned I became. Her husband's death had caused her to lose a fairly significant portion of her income. As she spoke of how she wished to live (and she was not an extravagant woman), I began to fear that there simply wasn't enough money. She too seemed to realize that money was going to be tight. I had the impression that she had come to my office hoping against hope that there was a solution. She seemed ready and willing to adapt in whatever way was necessary, but she had one very high priority, and she was searching for some way to maintain it if at all possible. Given her circumstances, it was a difficult one to meet.

Janet clearly understood that she would have to work in order to make ends meet, but it was her fondest wish to remain in the job she had had for a few years. It was a simple job that didn't pay too well, but she loved it. Even more important, it was providing her with a considerable amount of emotional support as she adjusted to life without Tom. She was very close with her coworkers. The job was fulfilling emotionally but not financially. I couldn't see how she could make ends meet if we didn't find a little more money somewhere.

And so, as financial advisers do, I began to look for some solution. I asked questions: Was there an asset that could be sold to generate more cash? Could she reduce her expenses somehow? Was there any money that could be used for income that we weren't considering? A certificate of deposit? A military retirement plan? Any life insurance? They stopped me there. Yes, in fact they remembered that there had been a small policy that they'd lost track of in all the concern over Tom's health. I brightened. Perhaps this was the solution. But neither Janet nor her children could remember exactly how much money was involved there. We made a few phone calls and finally got all the information on the contract. It was not an enormous amount of money, but it was enough to make the difference. It was enough, it seemed to me, to buy her freedom.

As we pushed and pulled on the numbers, the realization set in for them as well. Janet's son leaned across my desk and said, "Are you saying that if Mom's careful with this money and it's invested properly, she may have enough to live on and can stay in her job?" "Yes, I believe so," I replied. Then Janet leaned across my desk and repeated her son's question, as if she dared not believe it. "Are you saying that if I'm careful with this money, I may have enough to live on and won't have to change jobs?" "Yes, I believe so," I repeated. Janet leaned back in her chair with a big smile on her face. "Great!" she exclaimed.

Janet's "Spread-the-Joy" attitude toward money applied to everyone, and that included herself.

In my experience, this kind of clarity about one's money as well as one's priorities is somewhat rare. Like Cheryl before her, Janet saw money as a simple tool and used it in a way that promoted her healing. There was great grace in her relationship to her money and great peace.

In time, all of the financial tasks that follow the death of a spouse are completed. The budget and the investment portfolio are adjusted. Your financial life assumes its new rhythm. Hopefully all the work that has been done at this time paves the way for a peaceful and good life despite the loss. The goal in all of this reevaluation and reworking is to facilitate your new life, to put your financial house in order once again so that you can move on beyond at least financial concerns. It may not be pleasant to deal with your money after your spouse's death but it's vital to your future.

It may seem harsh to say it, but from a financial point of view, death creates opportunity. It creates a situation in which we can evaluate and improve our relationship to money if that's what's needed. The emotional challenge is great, of course, and the complications that finances present certainly add to the challenge. Taking over the family finances after the death of a loved one, especially that of a spouse, may be unfamiliar territory, a sad reminder of the person lost, but it's essential.

If you find yourself faced with this challenge, give yourself time to get back on your feet before you tackle the financial tasks. And then, as best you can, assume them with grace and calm. Money itself can be the tool you use to embrace this new phase of your life with its new identity. It will undoubtedly be a sad transition, but it can still be positive. It can be graceful. No matter what, life goes on. Money can be a positive part of this change, or it can be an incredible burden. As in all things, the choice is ours.

8.

RECEIVING WITH GRACE

There are few things that bring out the problems in a family more than the death of a family member with money! Like all of the other events treated in this book, inheritance is another form of "money in motion" that has both tremendous potential for growth and numerous traps. Although we're not accustomed to associating the idea of receiving money this way with personal challenge—what challenge could there be with a windfall?—it can raise a number of complicated emotional issues.

Inheritance has always been a major theme in the financial world, but over the next several decades it will become even more important. It makes up the first wave of money being transferred during this great shift of wealth that has already begun. Generally speaking, this is money that will pass from the current senior generation known for frugality and savings, to younger generations known far less for their sense of economy! It will pass from a generation that either lived through the depression or felt its effects very sharply to generations that have grown up and aged during a period of great prosperity in the United States. These very different circumstances profoundly influence our attitudes toward and our relationships to money. We will confront these and other influences as we inherit from the older members of our families.

The experience of scarcity and need that the depression brought about left a deep mark on America. Even today we still witness its effects when we hear people make statements such as, "We could never spend that money that Dad saved. He lived through the depression, you know." For people who lived through it, the depression was a defining moment in their financial lives.

Likewise the experience of prosperity that the baby boomers have enjoyed has shaped their financial thinking. There has been much discussion in the financial world about the fact that the savings rate has steadily declined in the United States. This certainly represents a number of things, but at the very least it represents a financial confidence that those who knew the depression never had.

Now as we embark upon the massive transfer of wealth already under way between these two generations, we have the opportunity not only to observe our very different relationships to money but, even more important, to shape our new experience.

Contemplating an Inheritance

There are many different ways to think about an inheritance. If you're about to receive one, your thinking is undoubtedly colored by your current financial situation as well as your relationship to the person from whom you will be receiving the money. You may be eagerly anticipating it, feeling gratitude and relief, or even, believe it or not, dreading it. But no matter what your circumstances, an inheritance is almost always a sort of a windfall. And a windfall can be a blessing or a curse!

As we contemplate an inheritance, most of us immediately think about the fun things we can do or buy with extra money. There's almost always something, either big or small, that a person would like to do with a little extra cash. That's the fun part of course. But sometimes this "extra money" can be tangled up with difficult family dynamics or an uneasy relationship to the person who has died. These feelings can easily taint the money being received. At other times, money that's inhcrited can come with strings attached that can be real (as in a provision in a will that restricts the use of the money until the recipient reaches a certain age) or psychological (as in, "Dad would never have approved of me spending this money!").

Some inheritances feel like a gift of love, an extension of the loved one. I have a client, for example, who lost his wife tragically after only a few short months of marriage. A few years later, when he turned sixty-five and visited the social security office, he was stunned to discover he was entitled to receive a portion of the social security payment his deceased wife had earned over her working life. This was a totally unexpected monthly payment that he was now to receive from then on. "She's still taking care of me!" he exclaimed fondly.

But there are others who think of an inheritance as their due. They look at their parents' money (if, in fact, they know the details of their parents' finances) and consider a portion of it rightfully theirs. They begin planning for it immediately and resent any spending that the parent does that might jeopardize their inheritance. An attitude of entitlement like this is, of course, very unbecoming to say the least. It also places a great burden on a parent. I have actually seen older people hesitate to spend money on their own care out of a fear of not leaving enough money to children who have communicated their desire for their fair share of inheritance.

The Value of a Windfall

No matter what your circumstances or your attitude toward an inheritance, it's almost always extra money in one way or another. It's special money, unlike our other resources, because it's largely unearned, because it often comes in a lump sum, and even because sometimes it's a surprise. In my opinion, this special status of "windfall," whether large or small, is very important. The very fact that an inheritance is separate and different from our other money ought to encourage us to step back and examine it differently. Inheriting money provides a fantastic opportunity, not only to do special things, but also to explore our relationship to our money in a relaxed and unusual way.

Handling inherited money—deciding what to do with it, how to invest it, and the like—is easier in many ways than making financial decisions in other types of situations. Perhaps because it *is* extra money, because it comes as a gift and is unearned, the stakes don't seem as high for many people as they do in the many other circumstances where money is involved.

Consider an inheritance in comparison with the other pools of money that you very well may need to deal with at one time or another. For example, making decisions about what to do with inherited money doesn't seem nearly as irrevocable as investing your retirement money. The money issues connected to an inheritance are not nearly as emotionally charged as the money questions people deal with when they're going through a divorce. Choices made regarding inherited money needn't be tinged with the kind of sadness that they often are when we take on the care of our elderly parents. With inherited money, we don't usually feel the heavy responsibility of making financial decisions for someone else. Handling inherited money is simply not as anxiety producing as making financial decisions in most other life situations. And that's the great thing about inheritance: It's one situation where we can be more relaxed and more creative. Very broadly speaking, inheritance tends to represent more opportunity than it does threat.

Put Your Money Where Your Heart Is

An inheritance of any size is a tremendous door opener and, for many, a once-in-a-lifetime chance to step back from their money. It's filled with promise not only for what good things we can do with it but also for the growth we can experience through it. To my mind, inheritance is more an opening for change and for growth than anything else. It can even feel like a miniature version of winning the lottery!

Much has been made on television and in the news of the gigantic good fortune of lottery winners. This type of enormous windfall fascinates us. It's dramatic and sudden; it changes a person's life forever. We imagine that winning the lottery would solve every problem we could possibly have, smooth the way through every challenge, and open the door to a totally new and far better life. It's the stuff of fantasy.

But we also know from many sad stories that a gigantic windfall like the lottery can also ruin a person's life. In part, this is because a lottery win is a public event. While this kind of money can definitely solve some problems, it can also create others. This sort of radically new financial status sometimes lands people in all kinds of trouble. Scam artists abound, bad habits worsen, and people sometimes just go a little crazy. In such circumstances, it's easy to lose sight of what's important. Of course, that's not what happens to everyone. For every lottery winner who falls apart, there's another who does not. Money is only a tool after all.

If we're looking for ways to sabotage ourselves, money can help us along very nicely. But if we're looking for growth and peace, money can help there too. For the vast majority of us, inheritance will not be as dramatic as the lottery. It's usually not as large or as unexpected or as public, but it too can be dangerous territory for those leaning toward ruining their lives. Or it can be the very thing that turns them in a brilliant new direction.

Inheritance invites us to calm consideration. It lifts our financial thinking away from our routine concerns and encourages us to think about loftier goals for our money and for ourselves. If we're at all interested in understanding what our values really are, our thoughts about an inheritance will reveal them. And then the inheritance itself hands us the tool we need to put our money to the service of those values. In short, an inheritance, more than other sums of money that require our decision making, enables us to put our money where our heart is.

The Emotions of Inheritance

This is not to say that receiving an inheritance is always easy. Although we don't often think of troubling emotions accompanying an inheritance, they can. There isn't necessarily the fear of running out of money or the fear of making a fatal error that we can experience in other types of money situations (although there certainly can be fear as we make decisions on what to do with an inheritance), but there can be some rather surprising emotional reactions.

It's not uncommon for an inheritance to be tainted by emotions surrounding the person who has died: love, anger, regret. If these types of emotions remain unresolved after the death of the family member, they could easily be attached to that person's money. I remember a client whose wife had died suddenly of a heart attack. For a couple years following her death, he let the money he'd received from her life insurance policy sit untouched. He simply couldn't bring himself to make a decision on it or deal with it in any way. To him, it represented only sadness and loss; he referred to it as "dirty money." Only after some time had passed, and only when his financial situation demanded that he access this money, was he able to do anything with it. Finally, he put it to work because he had to, but if he hadn't had to, it might have sat untouched his whole life. It was simply too emotionally charged.

It's not hard to understand how, when someone very close has died, inherited money feels a bit unwanted. Rarely have I seen people take joy in receiving money in such circumstances. When a spouse has died, for example, taking care of the money becomes one more burdensome task. It can be a bitter pill indeed, especially if the person who has died is the one who always managed the money.

I've also seen heirs look upon their inheritance with a sort of exhaustion. If they have cared for the now deceased person for a long time, or if settling the estate has taken some time, receiving money can seem quite anticlimactic. It can pale in comparison to all that has gone before it.

Some inheritors treat the money they receive with a kind of reverence. They hold it apart from their other resources. Sometimes, they invest it quite differently from the way they've invested their other money. To me, this underscores the unique nature of this money and our tendency to treat it differently.

Of course, not everyone approaches an inheritance slowly or reverently. Some heirs do eagerly await their money. More than once I've had clients bring their children into their financial dealing as they near death or even simply as they get older. This is usually so that the older folks can pass on financial responsibilities to someone else, put financial details behind them, and turn their attention to other things. They do it most often for their own security and peace of mind and also for assuring a smooth transition as they age. Of course, this is generally a good idea. It's very helpful to a family if at least one member of the next generation is familiar with the financial landscape. Most families take care of this easily, but I've also seen it backfire.

I remember a meeting with an elderly client who felt it was time to begin preparing for death and for the distribution of his estate. He brought one of his sons along in order to familiarize him with the family money. This was a family that had not discussed money much, and I gathered that the son knew very little about his dad's financial resources. My client had asked me to prepare a summary sheet for our discussion. We chatted amiably for a while, and then I passed the summary across the table to both father and son. As the father looked over the sheet pensively, I saw the son practically leap from his chair. He grabbed the paper and studied it intensely, surprise and greed equally spelled out on his face. Things went downhill from there.

In the case of this family, or at least this son, showing him a potential inheritance was a big mistake. He began to want it very badly and, according to my client, began to beg his dad for his share of the money. The son now saw his father in a whole new light and not a very happy one for either. Their relationship became all about this money. That one meeting proved a great disappointment to my client. He regretted it long after. It revealed to him an unfortunate side of his son that he hadn't fully acknowledged. It soured their relationship for the rest of the old man's life. It may be that the son was equally unaware of the response he would have to this potential windfall. I simply don't know since he was never again included in any of the discussions about this family's money.

A "Money-Is-King" attitude destroyed one man's relationship to his son as the old man neared the end of his life.

Although this story was a bit extreme, I suspect that many families have experienced some version of it. Far too many of us know the conflicts that can arise in a family when an inheritance is at stake. If the distribution of property isn't clearly spelled out (something to be discussed in a later chapter), arguments and trickery often ensue. Money fights that play out within families, or even sometimes in the courts, can be incredibly damaging. They can also go on forever.

Unfortunately, an inheritance can set the stage for the manifestation of some of our worst tendencies. Inheritance can bring out a greed and jealousy that make us suspicious of others and grasping in our dealings with family members. At other times, that same inheritance can push us to see ourselves as victims, to believe we've been shortchanged. To an angry person, an inheritance provides a weapon with which to punish family members for past wrongdoings, and the kinds of disputes that sometimes erupt over an inheritance can cause families to hold grudges that last for generations. Stepping into the fray of inheritance disputes without clarity and awareness is a dangerous proposition. Anyone who has experienced it once is likely to try hard to avoid it a second time.

This all sounds terrible, I know, but here's the good news: In my experience, these types of arguments aren't the general rule. Most people work hard to be respectful of the inheritances they've received or will receive one day. Many people seem to feel that with this type of money, there comes an obligation to the person who has passed it to them, a responsibility to do something special or honorable. But even for those who simply add it to their other monies, it's a special gift, and therein lies the great opportunity that an inheritance presents.

The Opportunity Inheritance Offers

For the purpose of our discussion here, I am assuming that an inheritance really is a sort of windfall and not money that we need to pay our monthly bills. I'm assuming that we can have the freedom to look on it as an invitation to dream. When we receive an inheritance, we have a golden opportunity to slow down and ask ourselves some long-term questions like these: What is it that we have always dreamed of doing but have not been able to fund? Might this inheritance begin to make that dream come alive? What values are most important to us? Are we expressing them with our money? Might this money offer us a way to express or promote what's most important to us?

It's very enjoyable to entertain these types of questions, but it's a rare individual who does it in a deliberate way. How sad! It's an exciting and creative process, a chance to imagine how we might express ourselves through our money. It's usually a very happy endeavor.

Over these many years of watching money change hands, I've had the privilege of seeing some inspiring and extraordinary approaches to inheritance. Some have used their new money to improve their family's life in a very specific way; others have reached out to their entire community; and some have sought to fulfill a highly personal dream. In every case, inheriting money has permitted these people to express their values in very concrete and visible ways.

Take my client Paul, for example, who valued education above all. To express this value to his family in the most concrete terms possible, he placed his entire inheritance into an education fund to be used by the whole family. He even went as far as investing the money in a separate named account that became the "Special Fund for Education" and was never to be commingled with the family's other assets. This money remained available to any family member who needed it, but only for the purpose of education.

As the manager of the fund, Paul watched over it and distributed it fairly to his children and grandchildren. He was vigilant in assuring that one person or two didn't receive all the money but that there was some equality in the distribution of the funds. He made sure that everyone in the family who pursued an education received some of the money and that it stretched as far as his grandchildren's generation. That Special Fund for Education expressed over and over his joy in learning and the hopes and ambitions he had for his family, but it also permitted all his family members to dream in their own turn by providing each of them with an education. His inheritance became their inheritance. It was never about money, always about what he valued most: education and his family.

> For a person with a "Spread-the-Joy" relationship to money, inheritance is a special invitation.

I'm sure that Paul had communicated the importance of education to his family many times and in many ways over the years, and probably his family members would have sought good educations with or without this Special Fund for Education. But his inheritance was an opportunity for him to put his money where his heart was and help his family at the same time. It was a gift that involved several generations in a very positive way. He really made his inherited money work long and hard. It spoke for him in a way that perfectly expressed his values and his love.

Paul's Special Fund for Education was a fairly simple yet effective way to put his money into service. I've seen other clients take a more complicated route to extend their own good fortune beyond their families and to reach out to their communities or to existing charitable organizations.

Several of my clients have used one form or another of what's called a charitable remainder trust. In this type of arrangement, money is placed into a trust for the benefit of a charity. The person donating the money can have limited access to it while still alive. Eventually, the principal of the trust will pass to the charitable organization named as the beneficiary of the trust. This is a far more formalized approach that works well when the values you wish to express line up well with those of a specified charitable organization.

Because this type of gifting is a bit more complicated, establishing a charitable remainder trust should be done with the help of a knowledgeable attorney who can help you determine if it is an appropriate strategy for you and, if so, work with you to draw up the document correctly. In addition, you must also work with a good tax adviser since the trust may entitle the donor to a number of tax advantages. Although you do maintain control of the money while you're alive, your gift is irrevocable and cannot be taken back. Should your interests change, however, you can change the charity or charities named as beneficiaries.

One family with whom I worked funneled an entire inheritance into such a trust in order to benefit a church that had been an enormous part of their family's life. In their case, the inheritance they had received was an opportunity to express gratitude in a way that had never been possible before. Their gratitude and their gift meant that other families would benefit perhaps in the same ways that they had for many years.

Clearly a charitable remainder trust should not be approached frivolously. However, all that said, it's a wonderful way to set aside money for your favorite charity (the beneficiary must be a qualified charitable organization) and also potentially take advantage of tax laws that favor charitable gifting. I've seen clients who have gone through this process express great joy in their giving. Oftentimes, it's a way of involving themselves with their favorite charity in very special ways. Their involvement also goes beyond their own lifetime since the gift doesn't actually pass to the charity until the donor's death. It's one of the many ways to communicate your values through your money and beyond the grave. And the inheritance itself can be the very thing that moves an individual or a family to such an expression.

Money is the bridge between our values and our material world.

I've even worked with families with deep philanthropic interests who take things several steps further. These families, whose own needs are well taken care of, put large amounts of money to work benefiting their community. They take a far more complicated path than that of the charitable remainder trust; they form a family foundation, a legal entity complete with a board of directors, bylaws, and annual meetings.

Forming a family foundation accomplishes a number of goals for these wealthy and generous families. First of all, the large inheritances that these types of families receive permit them to create the organizations they've always dreamed of. Because it's a family affair, they're able to involve their children in very productive ways. As their kids become old enough to participate in the work of the foundation, they are included in all the meetings and decisions. They become involved in the family's legacy of giving and get to see it from several angles. Because foundations receive requests and grant proposals from many different sources, the kids gradually become part of the deliberations about which projects to fund, how to evaluate them, how to follow them and hold them accountable. They become a part of the business side of giving as well as the emotional side. Eventually they take over the running of this family organization.

For these families, establishing a foundation is a way of passing their inheritance on to the entire community. It benefits their families to be sure, especially in the way that it involves every member in the business of giving, but it also gives them the opportunity to know their communities, the nation, or the world in a much more profound way than ever before. They become a major resource for improvement in the lives of others. And because a foundation can support many different types of projects at once, their reach can be very wide. For these families, a large inheritance becomes the vehicle for making charitable gifting a permanent part of their family for generations.

These are wonderful ways to use an inheritance but also somewhat complicated. Not everyone chooses to give an inheritance away, and not everyone looks beyond his or her own family in deciding what to do with inherited money. For many people, the majority perhaps, an inheritance is for the inheritors and those closest to them. Sometimes, an inheritance simply buys financial security by adding more money to the pot. More often than not, my clients have carefully folded inherited money into their overall investment strategy and simply left it there to grow. They don't spend it or give it away or anything else. Having this extra money available can mean safety and may provide priceless peace of mind. Maybe it allows them to entertain some possibilities for themselves that have seemed impossible before: to work a little less, to travel a little more, to pursue a special interest, to start a new business. Having extra money to fall back on encourages a person to imagine new things. Sometimes just knowing that extra money is there is enough to push a person to act on a dream. Money can be the safety net that enables a person to soar.

No matter the size of the inheritance or the decisions we make regarding it, one thing is for sure: Receiving an inheritance is emotional. Joy, gratitude, regret, and sadness—it's all there as we receive from those who have passed. What we do with inherited money is important, of course, but how we see ourselves in relationship to it is just as important.

Where to Begin

If you're about to receive an inheritance or if you even imagine yourself having one, you're now in a position to study and begin to understand your relationship to money. Answering a simple question or two with honesty is a good place to start. If you like what you see, great! If you don't, your inheritance may be the very thing you use to change.

No answer to these questions is wrong, of course. All answers are useful. Your reactions to money are what they are; so don't be afraid to look squarely at yourself and to answer these questions frankly.

Imagine now that you're about to receive money, an inheritance that really is extra for you. You don't need to live on this money at all; it's a windfall. *What is your first tendency, your first thought about this new money?* And, more important, *Why?* I'm not referring to what you think you might buy; I'm speaking of your gut-level reaction to the money itself and also the reason behind that reaction. For example, is your first tendency to lock this money up where no one, including you, can get to it? Or are you more inclined to show it off by buying things that display your new wealth? Is your inclination to spread it around generously, to share it with others? Or do you perhaps see it as a tool that will help you get a jump on other people?

No matter how you answer, you have a peek at the motives and attitudes that color your entire relationship to money. Whatever you see and feel in relation to this kind of money, this is your chance to mold the connection you would like to have. For those looking to improve their relationship to money, this is a time to think outside the box and try something new. It's not an easy thing to do, but it's not impossible either.

Let's say for example that your first response is to squirrel this money away so that no one can get to it. This response is quite common, even among the wealthy. But what is it really about? Sometimes this need to lock money up is just a way to be prudent. Sometimes, it's a way to be sure money is available at a later date for some special purpose. At other times, however, it belies a need for security and a fear of poverty that can dominate a person's financial life. Because financial advisers often deal with people who have enough money, you wouldn't expect that we see many people who consider themselves poor. And yet, there are those, even among the very wealthy, who think of themselves as poor, no matter what their balance sheet says. Although this attitude doesn't apply to the majority of people with money, it is a phenomenon that financial advisers see with some regularity.

I don't wish to be critical of people who experience this fear.

In my experience, most people who consider themselves poor have been poor at some time in their lives or they're the children of parents who knew poverty. The suffering from not having enough, from worrying about money, and from struggling is indelibly marked on them. Often it is this very experience of poverty that has driven these people to acquire wealth. They seek wealth because they know they don't ever want to be poor again. Making sure that they have enough money is very important, a direct and logical response to being poor, but may not be enough to quiet the fears.

This mind-set of "not having enough," of being poor, can dog a person no matter how much money he or she acquires, and it can be very difficult to change. No matter how much money is amassed, how much fortune built up, they continue to think of themselves as poor. I think that most people don't even recognize this deep-seated belief or consider the possibility that it can be altered. It's very stubborn indeed. And so, of course, it's perfectly understandable that they would want to tuck an inheritance away and have it available in case of that "rainy day." But observing this behavior in oneself and understanding how it plays out in our lives can be very valuable. Inheritance can be just the thing to reveal it.

The "Wolf-Never-Leaves-My-Door" attitude to money is a stubborn one indeed!

Folks whose belief in poverty is greater than their belief in prosperity immediately lock their money away in a safe place. They want to stock it up and hide it in order to ward off the terrible calamity that's always just around the corner. The good news is, however, that this is an attitude that can be altered. For someone who wishes to reshape his or her relationship to money, deal-ing with an inheritance provides a nonthreatening opportunity to experiment with a more expansive and relaxed attitude. It can be a time to explore the feelings that go with acknowledging that you have enough, that you needn't fear for your future, or that you could even give a little money away. And because an inheritance is "extra money," experimenting in this way needn't threaten a per-son's day-to-day financial life or long-term financial stability.

But some people with whom I've worked respond to an inherit-ance with the exact opposite of the "Squirrel-It-Away" approach. Some people go through inherited money very quickly. Their first inclination is to blow it all. Many an heir has spent an inherit-ance down quickly, almost without realizing it. Extra, unexpected money provides a license to be excessive and reckless. Here there's no long-term planning, only immediate gratification. Spending it quickly undoubtedly provides a kind of rush for these individuals, something that doesn't really bode well for their financial futures. But once again an inheritance can provide a needed opportunity to experiment with a different approach. If a person is willing, this can be a chance to step back, slow down, and explore how it feels to not spend, to be responsible with money, or to think beyond the immediate gratification of a purchase.

This type of reflection enables us to see quite clearly the ways in which our basic attitudes toward money play out in our financial life. In fact, it might even reveal tendencies that operate in many other aspects of our life. Sometimes, of course, these tendencies are constructive; at other times, they're not.

So imagine yourself once again about to receive a significant amount of money in the form of an inheritance. How does it make you feel? Are you suspicious? Feeling the need for secrecy? Afraid that others might learn of your newfound wealth and try to take advantage of you? We all want a certain level of privacy in our financial lives. But are your suspicions a normal part of our society's acceptance of this type of privacy or do they reflect a general distrust or fear of others?

Do you see yourself using your new money to hurt someone? This is the saddest of all. It's the "I'll-show-them!" tendency of those who use money to prove themselves or to make a point. This can involve a lot more than simply buying something fancy to show off to others. Subtler is the person who dangles new money before others and then deprives them of it or uses it to dominate them, hold them hostage, or show disdain. I've seen individuals take over the control of an inheritance specifically telling their own family members that they have done so because they believe that no one else would be as capable. I've seen them use an inheritance as an opportunity to dredge up and remind a family member of every financial mistake he or she has ever made. I've seen them withhold money from another, insuring that the other person remains dependent. For someone who seeks to dominate, money is an especially effective tool and inheritance too easy an opportunity.

> For someone with an "I'll-Pick-Up-the-Bill-If-You-Just..." relationship to money, an inheritance spells temptation.

These tendencies are very destructive, and hopefully not many of us are prone to them. You may like what you see very much when you imagine yourself receiving an inheritance. In my experience, the vast majority of individuals in this situation treat their new money with care and respect. They consider it a gift and are understandably appreciative. They use their money in a variety of ways to improve their own lives and the lives of those around them, consciously putting their money to use in a way that honors the person from whom it was inherited. Some launch new projects; others extend and amplify existing ones.

Inheritance should spell growth on many levels, from the most superficial to the most profound. But the extent to which it will be a true and meaningful opportunity depends on our willingness to observe ourselves and to be honest about what we see. Negative behaviors can be changed; positive ones can be expanded. Looking honestly at what a windfall like an inheritance brings up is a fruitful first step, not only toward a better relationship to money but also toward greater self-awareness.

At First, Do Nothing

To my mind, one of the first things a person should do upon receiving an inheritance is nothing at all. This is especially true if there has been no time to think about the money or if it's accompanied by some strong emotion. I often recommend to widows and widowers, for example, to allow insurance money to sit for several months in an interest-bearing account until the raw emotion that can accompany the death of a spouse has subsided a bit. There are simply too many emotional entanglements to allow for good decisions or clear thinking, and most people in that situation are not too inclined to focus on money anyway.

But even in a less difficult situation, it isn't a bad thing to allow the money to sit quietly while you contemplate it. Separate yourself from the money and spend a bit of time thinking about it. To begin to understand your basic attitudes and beliefs and to set the stage for the type of growth that a windfall can afford, you need to ask yourself questions that can be grouped into four general categories.

The first type will get you going in the right direction.

- How do I feel about this money? (happy, sad, fearful?)
- What kinds of things does this new money make me ponder? (running away? starting a business?)
- What are the kinds of things I might want to do with this money? (special projects? long-held dreams?)
- What might this money make possible that has been out of reach before? (travel? education?)
- What thoughts surprise me when I consider this money? (that I'm indifferent to it? that it scares me?)
- Do I feel differently about this money than I do about my other money? (I'm afraid to touch it? it feels more important?)
- What harm can come from this money? What good?

Once these questions have been considered, you can begin to narrow down what this money can really be used for. Again, more questions as you begin to dig into category number two.

- Given what I feel about this money, are there attitudes or beliefs I want to try to change? (a certain stinginess, for example, or a tendency to overspend?)
- Can this money be put to work on special goals that I have had to postpone because they were unaffordable?

- Can this money move me along quickly in a worthwhile direction I'm already going?
- Is there a problem in my financial life that this money can solve (retirement savings? care for another person? debt reduction?)

Perhaps you find that your attitude toward money is very constructive and that you don't really have any problems that need to be solved. Then an inheritance can be about your dreams. What could be more fun than to dream big and have some money to put behind that dream? Category number three gets more creative.

- In the best of all possible worlds, if there were nothing holding me back, what would I be doing for myself and for others?
- How can this money contribute to that dream?

Last, and perhaps most important of all, there is one final question to drive home a point about the potential for personal growth an inheritance offers its recipient.

- If what I did with this money and the ways in which I handle it were to be remembered long after my death by family, friends, and community, what would my decisions say about me?

Armed with all this reflection, managing an inheritance becomes much easier. A good financial adviser who is willing to listen to your thoughts, your concerns, your goals, and your emotions can help you accomplish what you seek with your money. The clearer you are, the easier your financial decisions become.

In our society we are not accustomed to thinking about inheritance as a problem, and for the most part it's not. But neither are we accustomed to thinking about how much of an opportunity it can be. Now, more than ever, is a time to expand our thinking about money to include these types of considerations. As this great shift in American wealth continues over the next several decades, many individuals will be in a position to explore, alter, expand, and improve their relationships to money. We are truly entering a time when we have a chance to change our very consciousness about money for the better, to see it as the tool it truly is. The task isn't an easy one, but the potential rewards, in our personal lives and in our society, are enormous.

III.

Money and the Legacy You Leave

W hat if the only way others knew us was by what we did with our money? If only our money—not our loved ones or our deeds—spoke for us when we were no longer here, what would the world think of us?

We rarely consider our money from this point of view, but the truth is that our money is always speaking for us, now as well as after our death. In my opinion, the true legacy we leave with our money is communicated less by what we leave behind and more by how we handle our money, how we think about it, what we use it for, what we teach our children about it, what example we give to others through our actions, and what we choose to do with it after our death. These actions, attitudes, and beliefs lay bare both our strengths and our weaknesses in more ways than our possessions ever will. For good or for ill, the principal emotional themes of our lives will shine through our money decisions with considerable clarity.

Our personal financial legacy has numerous components. Charitable gifts, foundations, large homes, and vast fortunes are all a part of it, of course, but these are the obvious elements of a legacy that are not available to everyone. Not everyone can afford organized charitable giving. Not everyone can amass a fortune. But everyone deals with money on some level. Everyone's emotions are somewhat entangled with their money. And so, each of us, whether it's conscious or not, leaves an imprint with and through our money.

Because money is so pervasive in our lives, we're given countless opportunities to explore our relationship to it and what that relationship says about us to others. Over and over we're invited to reflect on the meaning of money in our lives. And yet, for the very reason that money is such a presence in our day-to-day existence, we don't often stop to consider its deeper meaning. We take it for granted, and we absorb what the world tells us about our money with very little scrutiny.

What is the real meaning of our financial status? Is there any meaning at all? What does it mean to be poor or rich? Many in our society would say that wealth is a reward. But what if it's really a test? What if wealth is a lifelong opportunity to develop generosity or humility and has nothing to do with success? Could poverty, in fact, be a long experiment in dignity or simplicity or humility? In the view of eternity, of course, it doesn't matter at all if we're wealthy or poor, but it does matter how we live with our wealth or our poverty.

All of our money situations provide us a springboard for diving into these types of deeper issues. Whether our reflections come from big circumstances or small ones hardly matters. It may take us years to understand them, or we might grasp them in an instant. The important thing is that we open ourselves to all that money has to teach us and then begin to consciously cultivate our financial legacy.

Our financial and emotional heritage is very subtle. It's in the quiet and often unconscious messages we convey throughout our entire financial lives. The way in which we have handled our money, treated others in relation to it, what we have believed our money permitted us to do—all of this will speak of the most basic stance we hold in this world, our most fundamental outlook. Our legacies can be those of fear, entitlement, and avarice or of gratitude, compassion, simplicity, and generosity.

I do understand, of course, that money can't speak of all that we've been and that no one's life can be summarized by its money angle alone. Nonetheless, the financial side of our lives, a side so infrequently examined from this emotional or attitudinal point of view, does reveal a great deal about us. But the goal of Part III is to help you become aware of all you are communicating through your money and to encourage you to shape your financial messages consciously.

This may seem a somewhat frightening thought. Many people feel that money is largely out of their control, that they're the victims of their financial circumstances. Others find money too complex or too uninteresting a topic to warrant their attention. For whatever reason, these individuals choose to ignore money, but they are still communicating through it nonetheless. Other people, far too many of us in fact, allow ourselves to believe that we're controlled by money rather than to see it as a tool with which we can express almost anything we wish.

No matter what our circumstances may be, we're always in charge of the subtlest aspects of our financial life. At the very least, we're always in control of our emotional relationship to money, and that's the good news. Inasmuch as that emotional relationship is within our control, it can be adjusted. If our attitude is unhealthy, it can always be altered. If it's a happy and healthy attitude, it can be expanded. With awareness, our emotional relationship to our money can be shaped into whatever we wish it to be. And from there, the experience of our financial lives begins to change.

Two Opportunities to Fashion Your Legacy

Where then does the legacy we leave with our money begin? It starts, of course, with our own financial actions. It starts with all the attitudes, emotions, challenges, and victories described throughout this book. These tell our story just as surely as if we had put it down in writing ourselves.

In my opinion, however, we can go much further in thinking about the legacy we leave with our money. There are two areas of our lives that stretch well beyond our own lifetimes, two areas where we can and do extend ourselves without ever really knowing where our actions might lead. These two areas of financial life transmit our financial legacy in an especially vivid way. They are where our money will speak the most loudly on our behalf.

The first of these will not come as a surprise. It's our children. For most of us our greatest contribution to the world is the children we raise to be happy, productive, and honorable adults. They are the greatest mark most of us leave. No matter what we've accomplished in our own lives, most of us want more for our children. We all feel a sense of pride and take a little credit when our children do well. They are our legacy, for better or for worse. What we teach them about money will impact not only their own lives and those of their children but also all of society. Their money awareness, their attitudes, and their beliefs are part of our legacy.

Raising financially healthy children in the wealthy world in which we live can be a challenge. But to raise children with a strong and healthy relationship to money is also a great gift. Just as our children's successes make us proud as parents, so too should their positive emotional relationship to money. This gift to our children ought to be something we consciously seek and cultivate. It ought to be the most significant part of our financial legacy.

The second area where we can consciously create a financial legacy concerns what happens to our money after we die. This too is something that's almost entirely within our control. As we write our wills and trusts, as we go through the process of estate planning, we reveal ourselves one last time. Planning for what will happen to our money after we die is our last, and sometimes best, opportunity to allow our money to speak well of us. It can speak of our strength, our love, and our generosity. Or it can speak of our anger, our small-mindedness, or our need to dominate.

What does your money say about you? What legacy will you leave through your actions, attitudes, and teaching about money? As we enter this period in our nation's history, when more money will change hands than ever before, it's imperative that we ask ourselves these questions. More of us than ever before will find ourselves in the situations that beg them. More and more of us each day are being prompted by this great American transfer of wealth to contemplate our financial legacy. What an amazing opportunity we have before us! What a gift!

9.

HEALTHY KIDS IN A WEALTHY WORLD

Whatever issues we grapple with when it comes to money, we can be sure we're passing them down to our children. A very large part of the subtle legacy we leave with our money has to do with what we teach our kids about it. I refer here not only to what we know we ought to teach them about how to handle money—how to save, manage credit, invest, set a goal, and the like—but also to what we demonstrate to them by our own unspoken attitudes and our behavior. Are we teaching them to give money more weight in their lives than it deserves? Do we sacrifice our values for it? Are they watching us punish others with our money? Are we punishing them in some way? Do they see us use it as a weapon in any circumstance? Or do they witness and experience generosity, kindness, and freedom?

They learn all of these behaviors from us. They may, in fact, be picking up attitudes of which we're essentially unaware. Whether we care to admit it or not, in our society a very big part of a child's experience of growing up will include money. And we, the parents, will largely dictate the type of financial experience our children have as they grow. Until children have their own money to work with, they're learning the better part of what they know about money, and especially what they feel about it, from us. Raising healthy kids in the wealthy world we live in is a big responsibility!

And yet, what better way to leave a positive financial legacy than by raising financially literate and responsible children, kids with healthy emotional relationships to their money? Our kids are one of the best parts of our overall legacy in the first place. We owe it to them to prepare them to live in the financial world with grace and ease.

In addition to that, many of our children will be part of this massive shift of wealth taking place now and in the coming decades. They too will be faced with major decisions involving money, decisions where their emotions will run high and the stakes will be significant. In many cases, they'll handle these situations just as we have. They will have inherited our caution or our abandon, our wisdom or our ignorance. In short, they may very well display the exact same strengths and weaknesses that we have. Financial attitudes and behaviors are passed down in families. Think about your own parents, and you may well find that you are a financial "chip off the old block."

An Onslaught of Information

Young people today are bombarded with financial messages. Much has been made of the fact that advertising is being funneled to younger and younger children. Through television, the Internet, music, their peers, and, of course, their families, money weaves its way through a child's life every bit as much as it does an adult's life, although with some very different angles. There are now television programs, for example, targeted at a fairly young audience that focus almost exclusively on extravagant behaviors relating to money. These shows highlight the spending patterns—and only the spending patterns—of very wealthy individuals. They discuss the homes, the cars, the parties, and the wardrobes of celebrities. Although they sometimes give passing reference to some of the charitable interests and gifts of the celebrity in question, they're mostly about their consumption. Of course, these programs are fascinating to young people; the lifestyles presented are the stuff of fantasy. And I know that we're all a bit fascinated by lifestyles that are extravagant and considerably grander than our own. But my point here is that our young people can absorb a steady diet of this type of message about money if they care to simply turn on the TV.

But television isn't the only thing kids contend with. There's also commerce. When my own daughter turned eighteen, for example, I was stunned to see the number of credit card offers that began to pour into the house. Daily, we would shred multiple offers from banks and credit card companies all looking to extend credit to this young person. And the flow of offers hasn't subsided. In fact, it has increased. These offers were timed of course to come into the house when we were very focused on money. My daughter was preparing to head off to college, a season when many a family has long dinner-table conversations about college costs, family resources, financial aid, and part-time jobs.

It's easy to be critical of this practice on the part of the lending institutions. It's certainly a well-known fact that Americans carry far too much credit card debt and save too little. And yet, this is the reality that our kids will deal with. This is the real world they will enter. It's our job to teach them to enter it in a responsible and knowledgeable way. We need to help them be smart when it comes to money. Our job is to educate and to influence them in positive ways so that they step into the role of adults with clear heads and good financial habits. And it's not just that they'll inherit our money one day or that they'll have many of the same financial decisions to make that we have had. Let's face it: There's a good chance that one day we'll be in a position where we must rely on them to care for us. That may very well include managing our money!

What Our Kids Experience

From a very young age, our children are watching what we do with our money. They're observing our behavior to be sure, but they're also absorbing our attitudes and our beliefs. Perhaps our worry about what kids absorb from television programs is misplaced. Perhaps we should worry far more about what they absorb from watching us! If we argue over money, and lots of families do, they will understand that money causes stress and problems. If, on the other hand, they hear rational discussions about money and watch their parents as they make financial decisions, they will at least see the process play out in front of them. The decisions may or may not be the very best ones, but at least they'll know that money is something that can be discussed and that communication about money is a positive thing.

In some families, money is a secret. In these homes, money may be hidden or stolen, whispered about or quietly ignored. Who knows what the kids who live in this environment think about money? Do they see it as a source of embarrassment or confusion? At the very least, it must seem a great mystery and that's no gift to our children.

Some children have a money experience with their mothers that is very different from the one they have with their fathers. This isn't necessarily a bad thing if both parents have a relatively healthy relationship to their money. It may even give a child two different models to examine, appreciate, and experiment with. On the other hand, though, it can also give a child ammunition to pit one parent against the other. Parents need to be on the same page, if not in what they personally believe about money, at least in what they're teaching their children.

There are families that have truly deceitful money habits and sometimes bring children into the drama. Is one parent stealing money from the other? Is one hiding money from the other? If children are aware of such behaviors, they're learning a terrible lesson that goes well beyond the money itself. They're learning that deceit is acceptable, especially deceit relating to money, and that money is really about power. They're seeing that money can be used very effectively by one parent to control the other or to control his or her individual situation. We fool ourselves if we believe these things escape the awareness of our children. I truly believe that even if they don't quite understand what's happening with the money, children fully understand the basic dynamic here. They absorb the lesson.

Get Your Kids Talking

It's an interesting exercise to get your children talking about their own perceptions about money and especially how it relates to them. Do they perceive themselves to be well off or poor? What is it that makes them feel the way they do? If they perceive of themselves as well off, what in their experience speaks of wealth? Or if it's the opposite, what is it that they lack that makes them feel poor? Of course some of what they feel will be influenced by their peers and the possessions that your family has relative to those of their friends. If there's something that they would love to buy at the time you pose the question, something that you feel your family can't afford, they might be feeling quite poor indeed. But overall, these types of conversations can be quite revealing and may well afford you some insight as you think about what you want your children to learn about money.

Many parents are surprised to find that their children see the family's money situation quite differently from the way they themselves do. For example, you may be proud of what you've been able to provide for your family, understanding the kind of work it has taken. How disappointing then it would be to learn that your children feel poor! Your children may want things that you don't feel the family can afford, and that's always an unpleasant feeling for parent and child alike. (Of course, we do our children no favors by buying them things that we can't afford!) They might want a lifestyle that you have no interest in. If your children are unhappy with their money situation, they may blame you for how they feel, or you may blame yourself.

But, of course, it can also be the opposite. They may be perfectly happy with their situation. They may see the same successes you do and have the same aspirations. They may have sound values and a healthy perspective. If so, you most certainly can take the credit for that! Or you may find that things you wish you could provide for your kids but can't don't really matter to them at all. What a happy discovery that would be!

Despite the "risk" of posing these questions, this type of exercise can open up a very fruitful discussion. It's a great opportunity to get a glimpse of what your children think about money. It may give you insights into what influences their thinking both for the positive and the negative. It may also help you begin to understand and maybe even articulate for them their own emotional relationship to money.

Of course, you may also recognize yourself in their words. Their comments may reveal some of your own hidden motivations, and that can be uncomfortable. I have often thought that children have a way of saying out loud the things that we feel deepest in our hearts. At the very least, this type of general conversation about money is an opportunity for both you and your children to talk about what you all consider to be the marks of true wealth. It's a chance to discuss the ways in which money is important in your lives, how you've all grown into the perceptions that you have, and what things are more or less important than money.

I have a friend who had held a job for many years that paid him very well but required long hours and lots of traveling. As his kids got older, the job really began to wear on him. He never seemed to have enough time with his family, and, because his job was so demanding, he was tired most of the time that he was with them. The money was great, but the whole situation was burdensome to him. When another opportunity came along that required less travel, he was eager to consider it seriously. It looked like a good fit for his skills and experience level, but it didn't pay as well as his current position. He decided to take it anyway and was very excited about the prospect of more time at home. His kids, on the other hand, were horrified. Less money???

At first, he was disappointed that they focused so much on the money, that they didn't immediately see the benefits of having him home more. But he knew that deep down, they had missed having him around and that once they made the adjustments that the family would have to make to a slightly smaller budget, everyone would be happy. The situation gave him a chance to talk with his kids about what was important to him. They all worked on the new budget together so that everyone had at least some say in how extra cash would be used. It all worked out beautifully. First and foremost, he was able to be with his family more, and that made everyone happy. But beyond that, the children saw some important lessons—how to evaluate a financial situation, how to make a good decision, how to compromise, how to communicate, how to adjust a budget to a new reality. And he clearly taught his children a few things about the trade-offs made in the world of work. My friend was building his financial legacy as they thought all this through. He did a great service to his children not by giving them money but by showing them a mature and peaceful relationship to it.

Lessons Passed Down

Not every story, however, is as positive as this one. Sometimes the lessons passed from one generation to the next are so subtle as to be almost unidentifiable. This was the case with a client who often spoke to me of her parents' poor money management. She had vivid memories of arguments between her parents about money. One of her most unhappy moments as a child was coming home from school to discover that they had lost their home. All of the family's possessions were packed up in their old car. Her mother was in tears, her dad ashamed. As for the kids, they were frightened.

As an adult, she vowed to never experience such a thing and devoted much of her working life to making money and assuring that her family always had enough. It would seem that she had broken the chain of poor money management in this family until one unhappy decision on her part changed everything. She made one horrible and very risky investment decision that was completely uncharacteristic of her. It ended in her losing most of her money. I doubt that she would have ever characterized herself as a "Money Martyr," but she had sabotaged herself using her money just as surely as her parents had so many years before. For whatever reasons, and I'm sure they were quite complex, she was unable to break this unhappy family cycle. Like her mother before her, she found herself in tears; like her father, she was ashamed. The legacy of an unconscious and unhappy relationship to money had reared its ugly head in the next generation. And who knows how witnessing this unfortunate pattern might play out in her children's lives!

The "Money-Martyr" relationship is an easy one to pass on to our children. It can pass virtually unnoticed and truly take us by surprise.

It isn't just the next generation we should think about as we attempt to raise healthy kids in our wealthy world. In some families, money lessons are passed down through several generations. In our business, it's the "depression mentality" that we see most often rippling like a wave through several generations. It's not at all uncommon to hear people talk about their own attitude toward risk in terms of the experience of their grandparents. It isn't that they were raised by grandparents who lived through the depression, but their parents were. Fear of loss, distrust of the system, a need to stockpile money—these are all remnants of the depression that many families hold on to and pass from one generation to the next without ever noticing. I'm not trying to say that the depression wasn't a terrible experience and that the lessons learned during that dreadful time should be ignored now in the twenty-first century, but it's worth examining what form of those lessons still makes sense today. Do they match the economic conditions today and, in particular, an investor's personal situation? A better approach would be to examine those dramatic lessons and adapt them to new realities, to integrate the best examples of prudence, savings, diversification, and hard work into your family's financial life. This is quite different from what we often see, which is something along the lines of "I just need to put my money in a coffee can and bury it in the backyard."

I hasten to add here that not all of the lessons passed from generation to generation are bad. Some, in fact, are quite good. Many a family has displayed great pride in earning, saving, and providing for a family or a community. Many families have built family businesses that teach these lessons over and over to new generations as they take the business over to expand and develop it. Sometimes these lessons are quite subtle. They may not be spoken of at all. They can be simply a part of the culture of the family, a rich heritage of financial responsibility.

The Value of Money is all about becoming clear and aware when it comes to our money. And in my opinion, if ever we should want to become clear about our money, it should be for the sake of our children. If we face challenging money issues, do we really want to pass them on to our kids? If we want our children to accomplish more than we have, as so many parents do, wouldn't true financial literacy, as opposed to financial fears, be a significant contribution to their good? If we're wealthy, our children must learn to manage wealth. They must acquire some valuable skills that pertain to this special status. And if we're not wealthy, our children must learn to be good stewards of what money is available. We try to teach our children so many things, try to prepare them for adulthood in so many ways. Why should we ignore money, something that will course its way through every aspect of their lives, just as it does ours?

What Our Kids Deal with Changes Over Time

Children deal with money in different ways than adults do. In fact, we may have forgotten the financial issues that they deal with. The issues vary of course, depending on their age. We may not always fully understand or even recognize what the issues are for our kids. For example, how many of us have blurted out to our children something along the lines of the old adage "Money doesn't grow on trees!" But, in fact, when children are young, they might not know where money comes from at all. Think of what they observe. We go to a machine, put in a card, and take out money. It certainly must seem simple to a child. To a young child, the idea that money would grow on trees would seem silly. Of course money doesn't grow on trees; it comes out of a machine!

Until kids are earning their own money, they're pretty much dependent on others for what money they have. Think of what this situation would mean to you as an adult if you always had to go to someone else to ask for what you needed or wanted, always had to justify it? Is it any wonder that kids are master negotiators? Financially speaking, the youngest ones are at our mercy! (Please understand, I'm not saying that young children should be given lots of money to control, but at some point they must be given some so that they begin to understand how to make money decisions.)

As they get older, some freedom comes with earning power. Now the child's financial life begins to resemble that of an adult. There are choices to make. Some kids have specific responsibilities (like car insurance), and at this point some kids begin to contribute to family resources or earn their own spending money. Some are tackling very large responsibilities, like saving for college or maintaining an apartment.

The older the kids become, the more they're aware of the money of others. As they begin to have a sense of how much things cost, they also begin to understand that some people have more (when, in fact, they may only appear to have more) and others have less (when, in fact, they may only appear to have less). As kids enter this fragile stage where they become aware of what others seem to have relative to what they perceive they themselves have, we can only hope that they have a healthy relationship to money. It's very helpful at this stage of development if our children aren't burdened by fears, superstitions, and bad habits that have been allowed to develop or passed down from parents or others.

Finally they will be out on their own, either in college or in the work force or both. They're now putting into practice everything that you've taught them about money. That can be a happy or a frightening thought!

What Do We Need to Teach Our Children?

So what steps must we take in order to teach our children well and instill in them some good money habits? How do we approach this difficult area of teaching? Fortunately, there are some concrete steps that we can take to help create financially healthy kids. None of these need be too dramatic. They can easily be incorporated into our daily family lives. Money comes up often in a family's life; we'll have many opportunities to discuss it with them.

Your first step should be to *decide exactly what it is that you want to teach your children.* What are your priorities about money? What is it that you really want to communicate to them? It may be that you want them to fully understand how to live within their means in this world where credit is so easy and gets so many people in trouble. Or, depending on your past experience, you may be more interested in teaching them how to save, how to conserve what they have. For some families, generosity and responsibility for others are the most important lessons. In other families, it's all about investments, how money makes money and creates wealth.

Whatever it is that you wish to teach your children, it's probably colored by your own money experiences. If you've experienced poverty, building wealth becomes important. If you've always known wealth, then it may be conservation or responsibility to the community that carries more weight for you. In any case, it's important to think through the money lessons you wish to impart to your children.

It can be helpful to make a list of the things that are important to you and why. From there, you can think about your children and about what priority you would give to each item on your list. Chances are you'll be able to teach them everything on your list in one way or another, but what if you couldn't? What would be the most important lesson? Your second most important? and so on. You may want to focus on one priority with one of your children but on a different one with another child. You know your family best, so try to be realistic about who needs what.

Step number two is to *discuss these priorities with your spouse.* It's important that parents be on roughly the same page when it comes to the financial lessons they're offering their children. In fact, this kind of discussion can be very good for a marriage! It isn't essential that everyone feel the same about money—in fact, it's probably impossible—but it's a very good idea to discuss what you wish to teach your kids about money and the best ways to handle it with them. At the very least, you can hope that you and your spouse aren't seeking to impart opposing lessons.

If your children are old enough to discuss it with you, the next step is to *find out exactly what they know and don't know* about money and also how they feel about it. There are lots of worthwhile questions to ask them in order to understand their point of view. Where do they think the family gets its money? What do they think are the most important things to do with money? Do they understand what money goes into the running of your home? Depending on the ages of your children, some of this could be over their head, but you can still adapt these types of questions to match their understanding.

From there you can dream a bit with them. *Ask them what they would do with more money if they had it to control.* This will give you an idea of what's on their mind. Ask them what role money plays in their life and what types of experiences they've already had with money. Ask them what things they observe about the money that they see other people spending. You might be surprised at what they tell you here. It will give you a glimpse of their money world outside your home, the world of their peers. This is especially important with older children, of course, where peer pressures can be such a significant part of their life and have such influence on their money decisions.

And, finally, *ask them what role they see money playing in the life of your family.* This too could offer some surprising answers. Your children might be aware of some interaction between family members that you're not aware of. They may understand your emotional relationship to money better than you do yourself. They may even see a side of your marriage that you haven't examined.

Once you have a better sense of their understanding of money and their thoughts about it, you can look again at the lessons you have set as priorities for your children. Is what you thought should be the most important thing still the most important, given what you've learned about them? Are there different things you need to emphasize? Or are you right on track with your priorities?

How to Impart Money Lessons

Now, armed with more knowledge about what your children already understand, you can begin to work out how best to teach your children about the world of money. Let's say, for example, that what you really wish to impart to your kids is the value of work and the ability to delay gratification. Simple exercises can begin to give your children the right idea.

When my daughter was about six years old, I remember that there was a stuffed animal she really wanted. We discussed the cost of this little toy and why she wanted to have it. We decided that she would need to save five dollars toward the purchase of the toy. At the time, five dollars seemed an astronomical amount of money to her. She had no sense of how much that was or how she could possibly earn that much. So I gave her a quarter and asked her to take a clean piece of paper and trace it twenty times. We put that sheet of paper on the refrigerator. Then we made a list of jobs that she could do that would each earn her a quarter. Each time she did one of the jobs, I gave her a quarter, which she put into a little bank. Then she drew a line through one of the quarters that she had drawn on the paper. It took a little while, but eventually she had twenty quarters and she had crossed out each circle on the paper. With a great sense of victory, we went to the store and bought the toy. She was thrilled! And I was pretty happy myself. In one little game, she had had a lesson in relating work to money, in delaying gratification, in setting a goal, and achieving it. We'd even gotten to throw a little math in there too!

Variations of this exercise work well with older children as well. Many a parent has offered to match what a teenager earns toward the purchase of a car for example. The more the child earns, the better the car. The key is to make the entire exercise as enjoyable and relevant as possible, to involve the children so that the goal and the reward are their own and are meaningful to them.

The lessons you wish to teach your children might be a bit different from these basic ones, though. What if, for example, you wish to promote generosity in your kids? Then you can find a project that encourages them to save and to give.

One of my clients who is the father of school-age children requires them to divide their money into three compartments. The first is the money that they're to save for future use. Then there's the money that they get to spend on whatever they choose. And, last, there is money that's to be given away to someone who needs it more than they do. He's involved with them in making the decision about what to do with this charitable money although it's largely up to the kids. It's important that the cause be meaningful to them. This way he insures that they remain somewhat involved with the giving and also stay committed to it. As a result, his children have developed a great appreciation for all they have and an ease in giving at a very young age.

Years ago I worked with a client who owned a family business that was located in a poor part of town. Each day the family would drive through this area on their way to their business. Their daughter, who was rather young, was rarely with them on these drives, but then she got older and entered those early teenage years when kids begin to be more aware of the world around them. One afternoon, this couple took their daughter out for a little ride. She protested that she didn't want to go and wondered where on earth they were headed. They quietly drove with her to that poorer part of town. There was a bridge there beneath which many people lived. This young teenager saw whole families there, including some kids her own age. She had no idea that there were homeless people in her town (and I suspect that many adults didn't know about them either). She hadn't ever imagined that kids could be in that situation. It made an indelible mark on her. It made her quite a bit more grateful for all that she had then and has now. She has grown into a very caring and generous adult. A powerful lesson that required so little.

> If you're a person with a "Spread-the-Joy" relationship to money, it's easy to teach your kids generosity. It can start when they're young and continue right up through the teenage years.

What if the lesson you care to impart concerns the power of advertising in making us spend our money? What if you want to teach your kids to be independent of what the advertisers (and their own peers) say one ought to own? This is a tough lesson to teach. A parent can easily seem quite out of touch to a child on this one. But I have known families who have a clever way of teaching their children about this. They make a deal with their kids that they will pay for a basic item, jeans for example. The cost of a basic pair of jeans, not the high-end brand name, might be fifty dollars. That's how much they are willing to pay. In addition to that though, they give each of their children a certain amount of money every month with which they can do as they please. If they want to buy the more expensive jeans, the hundred-dollar or even two-hundred-dollar ones, they can take the additional money from their very finite accounts. These people report that initially each of their children used much of their monthly money to buy the more expensive brand-name item. Rather quickly though, they become more selective and more careful with their money. The brand name gradually becomes less important than the freedom of having some discretionary money. Giving them the choice and showing what the brand means in terms of the cost of the item are the points of the exercise. A great approach and healthy for everyone!

The important thing in all of this is to be conscious and deliberate in all of our money dealings with our children. That leads us directly to the next step we can take: frank money discussions. How are our children to learn about money if we don't discuss it frankly with them? But some families are very secretive about money. Not only do they not want outsiders to know about their money dealings, but they also don't want each other to know. In this kind of atmosphere, it's very difficult to teach children anything too useful about the real world of money.

Other families are very open, however, and, to my mind, this is a far better approach for our children. It can be a very good thing to openly discuss with our kids the money decisions that most affect them. Of course, not everything needs to be discussed. But as things come up that have an impact on their lives, you have an opportunity to show them just how decisions are made, what considerations come into play, how compromises are reached, and why.

If, for example, your children want to have something that isn't affordable, explain that to them. If it's a good thing that you'd like them to have, help them figure out a way that they can contribute to its purchase. If it's something you don't want them to have, that should be explained as well. Show them what your priorities are.

They may not agree, but at least they'll understand. Far too often as parents we slip into a defensive mode here. Instead of discussing rationally, we get angry and feel our kids are draining us. Or we get frustrated and feel we're not doing our job. Or we feel unappreciated for all we have been able to do. But every family has financial realities. If we can make our children understand them, we all will have a better time of it.

Several years ago I took a trip with my kids on a fairly strict budget. I talked with them about how much we had to spend. At first it sounded like a great deal of money to them, and they were excited. But then we subtracted out the cost of a flight, the hotel, and our food to see what was left for play. Although they seemed a little disappointed at first, it gave them a clear sense of what was available. We had fun dividing up the available money and deciding what to spend it on. I don't think that showing them the budget dampened their spirits at all. And it certainly made for a more relaxed time for me.

Another useful step is to make your children part of family projects that involve money, especially as they get older. When a decision that involves money is being made, allow them to be part of the discussion. Allow them to have input. You can even make them responsible for some of the duties. Let me offer an example.

One of my clients recently decided to take a major vacation with his family. They planned and saved for this for some time. From the beginning, his school-age kids were part of the decision-making process. They all talked together about where they would go, what they wanted to do. That was the dream part of the planning. They decided on Disney World. Once they knew approximately how much they could spend, he helped his children to draw up a simple budget for the family. Together they got online to investigate travel packages. They looked at the most expensive ones and all that they offered as well as the less expensive ones and their features. They all discussed together which package gave them the most of what they wanted to do and still fit into their budget. The kids began to save their own money for this trip so that they'd have more spending money. They talked and planned and enjoyed every minute of the preparation. But unlike many families that plan trips and vacations, they made money an easy and natural part of the discussion. As you can imagine, when it came time to go, they were ready, and they had the time of their lives. The budget was clear, the activities planned. It all went beautifully.

Another way to include your children in discussions concerning family money may involve your professional advisers. If, for example, you work with a financial adviser on an investment strategy and a portfolio, it can be a good idea to include your children in an occasional meeting with them. Although this would be lost on younger children, as your kids near adulthood or get to an age where they're beginning to really understand how money works, it can be a valuable lesson for them. It's a way to not only teach them about finances but also introduce them to some of the responsibilities that they will assume later on. Advisers are usually happy to include your children, although it's a good idea to discuss this with them ahead of time. Your adviser will certainly want to know what you have on your mind as you include your children in financial discussions.

In this context, let me add a word of caution on behalf of advisers everywhere. If you care to involve your children in your discussions, please don't ask your adviser to do your job. We can teach about the things that we deal with, such as investments, for example. We can explain the strategies that we're using with family money if you wish us to, and we can certainly help a young person get started in investments. But sometimes our discussions with our clients are in depth and highly personal. If you wish your children to be involved, try to work out the ground rules for that discussion ahead of time with your adviser. It's only fair to your adviser to agree upon the kinds of things that you would like to see covered and whether or not there are any things that you prefer not be discussed with your kids.

The Question of Allowance

Personally, I believe it's important at some point that children have control over at least some money. It's great to discuss things with them, but it's no substitute for real hands-on experience. There are so many lessons to be learned as they actually make decisions with a bit of money. Making a mistake or two at an early age isn't necessarily a bad thing, and feeling the sense of independence and responsibility that comes with managing money can be very empowering. This, of course, brings us to the question of allowance.

There are different schools of thought on this topic. Should your children receive money for doing chores at home? Many people feel that this is a good lesson, linking money to work and encouraging them to contribute to the family. Others feel that chores are just a part of family life and that no compensation should be offered for doing one's share of them. In these families, an allowance is simply a sum of money the children are given to manage for themselves. For the parent doling out the cash, however, that can start to feel a bit uncomfortable. Obviously a child's allowance is one of those things that spouses need to discuss together and make a joint decision on.

Some families find a middle ground here. This comes in the form of extra work, above and beyond the routine family chores, that a child can do to earn some extra money. This approach ties money to work, which many parents like, but also avoids the trap of making a parent feel taken-for-granted. And it has the added bonus of accomplishing a few of those nagging chores around the house that never quite seem to get finished.

No matter how you handle the question of allowance, the important thing is that, at some point, children experience the responsibility for a bit of their own money. It doesn't have to be a great deal and, of course, much depends on their age, but this is where they can experiment with spending and learn how to make choices. This is where they realize that they don't have an infinite amount of money and that it can be used up pretty quickly or saved up for a special goal.

When I first began to give an allowance to my oldest child, I gave her a short list of items that I would no longer buy for her. If she wanted any of those things, she would need to use her own money. The very next day, we were in a drugstore where she spied a little notebook that she felt she needed. She asked if she could get it, and I told her that it would need to come out of her own money. If she wanted it, she could go ahead and get it; the choice was hers. At first she seemed exhilarated by the sense of freedom and control and then somewhat confused. She held that notebook in her hands for a long time and studied it. Finally, she tossed it back on the shelf and walked away. "I don't need it," she said. What a lesson!

Of course, if your children are given money to control, they must be allowed to make mistakes with it. If they spend it all quickly, then it's important that they do without for a while. (Now, of course, I'm not talking about the essentials, like food and shelter. I'm talking about the extras that they enjoy.) If they blow their money in the first week of the month, then they're out of money for the month. To be worthwhile, these exercises need to be real-life experiences.

It's interesting what you discover when your children first begin to control some money. I found that my son had an attitude and approach to money that were completely different from my daughter's. While she would save and distribute her money evenly over the many things that she wanted to use it for, he would focus on one thing. He would save his money to buy one item and ignore everything else. If it meant that he didn't have money to go out to eat with his friends, he didn't care. He was very focused on one priority. She, on the other hand, had several. Both of these approaches are fine. Managing their own money gave them a sense of their own financial priorities. I also saw a new side of each of them as I watched them handle it.

The Issue of Credit

Allowance is one issue for children over which you have a great deal of control. Credit is quite another thing. The reality in today's world is that kids must know how to use credit and debit cards. They will be inundated with offers of credit that make it all seem so easy. This is simply how most of us shop today, and so we owe it to them to teach them how to use credit and debit cards properly. Personally, I feel it's best to begin with a debit card tied to a bank account. They learn how to understand a bank account and at the same time how to access it and balance it using a debit card. It's very much like learning how to manage a checking account was for me when I was younger. They keep track of what they have in the account by keeping a ledger and checking their balance at an ATM. They use the debit card just as we used checks. It doesn't take too many of those high fees that the banks charge when you've overdrawn your account to encourage a child to get control and keep track, but they need to learn the mechanics of the system.

Credit cards are a different matter. Young people begin receiving credit card applications the minute they turn eighteen. These offers encourage them to have credit cards in order to "establish a credit history." My personal take on this is that there will be plenty of time for that later. I want children to get a good sense of managing the money they do have, living within the budget that they've set, saving a little, and meeting their financial responsibilities before they take on credit.

We all know that credit cards are one of the most expensive ways to borrow. Young people need to understand first of all that that's what they're doing when they use a credit card. They're borrowing money. And when they make a payment to the credit card company, they're paying it back, often with a great deal of interest added on. This may seem simplistic, but I think sometimes we forget that this is what credit cards are all about. We must teach our children to keep track of what's being charged on a card for a given month and to never charge more than they can pay back at the end of the month. They must also be shown how easily credit card debt can mount up and how hard it is to pay off.

You can teach children a great deal simply by showing them your own financial life. When you're paying a credit card bill, for example, discuss it with your children. By showing them the statement, you can teach them about the interest that's charged and the high cost of borrowing this way. These are not complicated things. Sometimes a simple explanation is enough to give them a basic understanding of the mechanics of credit card use. It's important not only to warn them of the dangers but also to show them the advantages of using credit, because the simple truth is that they will undoubtedly use it one day.

But before young people tackle using a credit card, they need to learn how to manage their own money. They should understand a basic budget and how to live within it. In this way, they're more likely to see a credit card as a convenient way of spending money that they already have (i.e., never charging more than they can pay off at the end of the month) instead of seeing it as a way to obtain extra money when they don't have enough to buy what they want. They're less likely to get into trouble by running up this very expensive form of debt.

Of course not everything about credit and debt is bad. There are situations where a little debt is unavoidable. Many people need to borrow when it's time to fund a college education for a child, and often it's the students themselves who do the borrowing. While we certainly hope not to burden a young person with unnecessary debt from their college years, at least this type of borrowing has some advantages. College presents a good opportunity to teach your children about borrowing and how to do it wisely and responsibly.

Many studies have shown that young people who take advantage of low-interest-rate educational loans are far more serious about their studies. These loans are available to most students and are an excellent way to teach a young person exactly how a loan works. The students are charged interest on the amount borrowed (although at a very low rate and, for some students, not until they've completed their studies). They have a set period of time during which the loan must be repaid. They receive regular statements so they can see exactly how the interest is charged and how any payment reduces the debt. And, as with all loans, they must make application and meet certain requirements. I'm certainly not recommending that students take on lots of debt in order to fund an expensive education, but, handled wisely, a small amount of this type of debt can be instructive.

Teaching Values and Money

Few of us have unlimited amounts of money to spend, and, even if we do, we all set priorities with our money. So why should we not share these to some extent with our children? Showing our children the ways in which we have applied our money to the things that matter the most to us can teach them quite valuable lessons. If, for example, education is a high priority and you've made sacrifices to afford the best possible education for your kids, then that's something to be discussed with them. Have you lived in a smaller home in order to afford education? Have you taken less lavish vacations in order to provide educational opportunities? Have your vacations centered around educational opportunities? These are the types of financial realities that we shouldn't be afraid to expose our children to. They show the ways in which we've put our own money to the service of our values. They demonstrate a process for doing just that, a process that the children themselves can use one day in their own families. The goal here is certainly not to play the martyr with them or provoke guilt; it's simply to share with them a bit of your own financial thinking and how it has gotten your family to the point it's at.

Although most of us don't relish it, it isn't such a bad thing to discuss the mistakes we've made with money either. I've found with my own children that when they've made mistakes that cost them some of their hard-earned money, those lessons have been strongly imprinted on them. The same is true for many of us. Why not share at least a little bit of information from the lessons we've learned the hard way? (This assumes, of course, that we have learned our lessons and have not continued to repeat these mistakes!)

Retirement Planning

Once your children are older and beginning to plan their independent life, it's time to help them think longer term with their money. When I began my first job, my father sat me down to talk about the benefits package that my new employer offered. I didn't have a thought in my head about things like retirement packages, but he impressed upon me that it was worth my time to have a look. I still remember him saying rather solemnly, "These things are put in place for everyone. You get to participate in them too. You owe it to yourself to study up!" He considered it a privilege and a responsibility to take the benefits package seriously. And so, as I was mostly just happy to have a job and to be out of school, he had me examining things like disability insurance! Of course that wasn't of much interest to me at the time. But in the area of retirement planning, he did me a great service by helping me get started with savings at an early age. Now, all these many years later, I consider it a special opportunity when I can talk to a young person about contributing to an employer-sponsored retirement plan because I know how powerful that can be over time.

Your children may be no more interested in this kind of long-term planning at a young age than I was, but if you can get them going with even a small amount of serious investing, it could really pay off for them. The objective is to encourage them to get started with savings and to learn to live on less than they're bringing home. These habits will stand them in good stead for years to come.

Exploring Their Money Relationship

And, finally, there's one more step that is, to my mind, the most fun part of all of this. Each new money experience we have with our children is an opportunity to explore that all-important emotional relationship, to get our kids talking about how they feel about their money and why they take the actions they do. Let's say, for example, that they find they're afraid to spend their money, that they hoard it, or that they simply can't make decisions about it. These are wonderful topics to explore with them. Are they afraid of the responsibility, fearful that they might make mistakes? Do they not want their friends to know they have some money? Are they afraid there will never be any more if they spend what they have now? Whatever it is, you can help them begin to understand the relationship they have to their money. You can teach them to explore it rather than fear it.

How many of us have learned our money lessons the hard way and sometimes with serious consequences! Including the emotional side in our teaching about money is something I believe we owe our kids. It takes the idea of financial literacy one giant step further.

Leaving an Inheritance

There is another more philosophical issue that relates to how we handle money with our children. It involves the question of inheritance and preparing an heir to receive and be responsible for inherited money. If your children are likely to receive an inheritance, especially if it's a sizable one, this too is part of your responsibility to them.

There is a basic philosophical question, though, as to whether or not you should even leave money to your children. Many people automatically assume that they should want to leave an inheritance to their children. They never really question the idea that anything that's left over at the end of their life should go to their kids. There's nothing wrong with this assumption, of course, and it's exactly the way many families plan it. Some parents see an inheritance as an extension of their own offerings to their children. They see it all as part of the continuation of the family, and in many wealthy families it's a given that the children will take over the family fortune one day.

But there are other individuals who question this premise. For them, there's a fear that leaving money will rob their children of the drive to make it on their own. They fear that their children will never appreciate what they have if they don't earn it themselves. These parents want their children to know the feeling of accomplishment and victory that comes with financial success attained on one's own.

Obviously this is something that families must decide for themselves. No one can tell you what's right or what's wrong here. A great deal depends on your own needs, on those of your children, and the size of your estate, but it's a worthwhile topic to reflect upon. Do you want to leave your children money? In your opinion, does this do them a disservice or does it give them a leg up? Do you prefer that they make it on their own, or do you want to help them avoid some of the struggles you might have experienced?

The majority of the people I've worked with do want to leave their kids money if there's any left over at the end of their life. Their first priority is taking care of themselves, of course, then providing a little something for their children. But this isn't everyone. I've also worked with families who have reservations about leaving money to children, especially when they're young adults. They fear that it might be a deterrent and encourage reckless behavior rather than responsibility.

All of this depends upon the individuals involved, of course. If you have enough money to leave an inheritance, you probably have an idea ahead of time about how your heirs will respond to their gift. It's part of our responsibility as parents to prepare our children to receive this inheritance if one is in the offing. Hopefully, little will be needed if you've taught your children when they were younger. But if you have some concerns, the good news is that it's never too late to start. Even adult children can be prepared for an inheritance through some good conversation and advance planning.

Some families choose to put restrictions on access to inheritance. The most common of these is related to age. Many people stipulate through their trusts that younger heirs can only have a portion of their inheritance at a certain age, then another portion at an older age, and so on. This is simply to assure that some of the money they're leaving will be available as their children reach different stages of their lives.

Many parents begin to include their older and even adult children in discussions with their financial adviser precisely to prepare them for an inheritance. This is especially important where there is a significant amount of money or if there are some special family projects or endeavors that the child will assume responsibility for.

Ultimately if you choose to leave an inheritance to your children, I believe you must consider it a gift. It's not a bad thing to build in a few safeguards to protect the money, but, at the end of the day, it is a gift. Our children will do with it what they will. If we have taught them well, they will use it in positive ways.

Whatever it is we care to teach our children about money, whatever we choose to do with it at our death, it's our job to encourage our children to develop a healthy relationship to money. If we teach them how to earn, how to spend responsibly, how to respect money without worshiping it, we will have done a good job. If they can go on to make sound financial decisions with ease and use money in ways that enhance their lives and the lives of their families and communities, we will have been a success. We will have given them a tremendous gift to carry them through their own adult financial lives with grace. They, in turn, will pass their financial wisdom on. Our legacy as well as theirs will grow.

10.

CONTROLLING FROM BEYOND THE GRAVE

Deciding what's to happen to our money after we're gone and thus contemplating our own death isn't much fun. I feel certain that's one of the reasons so many people put off estate planning. And yet, might we not be more enthusiastic about it if we thought of it as one of our last opportunities to right the wrongs of the past, create peace, communicate our values, and grow both personally and spiritually? The truth is that how we arrange to have our money distributed after our death can be one of our last and strongest statements.

At first blush, estate planning seems an awfully complicated process. This is especially true if the estate involved is large and spread out. Many people, including many financial advisers, think of the whole thing solely in terms of tax planning. For them, the principal goal is to arrange an estate in such a way that it passes to heirs with the minimum amount of taxation. There's nothing wrong with this approach of course. Reducing estate taxes is a worthy goal in and of itself, but in my opinion it just doesn't go far enough.

Planning for the distribution of an estate also involves other issues that can be very significant in the life of a family. It can go much further than the obvious questions of who is to receive money and how much, who is to be given what possessions, or what charities are to share in your wealth. There are many more subtle issues that come into play under the broad heading of estate planning, and many of these touch on some very basic elements of our emotional relationship to money.

There's a great deal involved in estate planning that can be quite sobering. Naming a guardian for minor children, for example, or deciding when your adult children will be ready to inherit money are two of these issues. There are also health-care choices to make as you prepare instructions on how you will spend the very last stages of your life, planning for a time, for example, when you and/or your spouse may no longer be able to care for yourselves. Understandably, few of us enjoy contemplating these things, but how you handle these questions can have a significant impact not only on your life but also on your family. The estate plan document you put together will guide them as they make difficult and worrisome decisions on your behalf.

A poorly thought-out estate plan can have serious fallout for a family. Depending on its contents, it can cause them uncertainty as to what's to happen and a great deal of potential confusion. Worse than that, it opens the door to and even promotes all sorts of arguments and conflicts. It can encourage your family members or other heirs to focus on your money in all sorts of unpleasant ways at a time when they may prefer to be focusing on each other or on you and your life. In a case like that, where ambiguity or even intentional poor choices cause arguments, conflict becomes a part of the legacy you leave with your money, and it can mark a family for years to come.

On the other hand, a well-thought-out plan is a beautiful gift to your heirs. It will facilitate an easy transition of your money and other possessions. It can communicate the care, concern, and respect that you have for them and mean that, at the time of your death, your family will be able to focus on things that will undoubtedly seem more important than money.

Unfortunately, many of us resist committing a serious estate plan to writing or even thinking one through. It's true that it's a detailed and, frankly, fairly tedious task. Yet, behind all the paper-work and the obviously unpleasant exercise of contemplating your own death, lies a great opportunity. Deciding how your estate is to be distributed is also about reflecting on the legacy you're leaving with your money and considering the statement you wish to make through it. It's one of your great opportunities to give concrete expression to your values. In short, it's a creative way to think beyond yourself and your own life. As in many of the money issues discussed in *The Value of Money*, the opportunities for good and for growth embedded in this endeavor are significant. And like all of the other life events that we've discussed, it too contains numerous emotional pitfalls.

All-Out War

Even though most people don't draw up their estate plan when they're at death's door, there can still be a sense of urgency about the whole endeavor. Perhaps it seems such a weighty operation because, unlike in other areas of life, you won't be around to correct any mistakes. On the contrary, all mistakes will be solidified in a legal document. The process is one that requires lots of reflection and needs to be revisited often over the years as your situation changes or as your wishes do. Without some genuine soul searching and, I would add, some compassion, wills and trusts can set the stage for all-out war!

Ronald was a client who exhibited an extreme example of the "I'll-Pay-the-Bill-If-You-Just…" relationship to money. He didn't have a huge portfolio but one large enough that he felt certain there would be some fights over it after his death. His health was very poor, and so he was eager to get his affairs in order. Each time I met with him—always at his home since he was too ill to come to my office—I was struck by the heaviness and darkness around this man. He was deeply unhappy, and that energy seemed to radiate throughout his entire house. Although he was always courteous in dealing with me, he was bitter and harsh when he spoke of others.

In order to arrange his financial affairs, Ronald had structured a trust document to clearly spell out what was to happen to his money after his death. In this trust, he systematically gave money to some family members and, just as explicitly, excluded others. In addition, he named distant relatives to oversee the distribution of his money, believing that they would be more objective and less susceptible to pressure from angry family members. This, of course, served only to increase the number of people involved in what even he seemed to feel would be a free-for-all. He clearly spelled out not only how much money individuals were to receive (unequal amounts) but also at what age they were to receive it.

This is not an uncommon practice in estate planning when children are involved but somewhat unusual with middle-aged beneficiaries. Although I had met some of his family members, I hadn't met them all. I assumed that this was a family with a long history of arguments, but I could also see that Ronald's instructions went well beyond any history of family disputes. He clearly wasn't trying to rise above the arguments or even settle them with this document. On the contrary, he was fanning the flames, insuring that he would remain part of the war long after his death. He was making sure that his family's disputes didn't end any time soon.

For Ronald, forging this trust was like swinging an ax. Although he said that the inequality of his gifts was intended to protect some family members and assure their financial future—and I have no doubt that on some level it was—clearly it was also to punish others. He used his trust document to express one last time his anger and his bitterness.

The effect of all of this was that Ronald solidified in a trust agreement the very divisions that existed in his family and thus insured that, at his death, brother and sister would be pitted once again against each other, mother and son would again play out their old arguments over this new issue. In fact, after this gentleman died and his heirs began to sort out his estate, the real ugliness of the situation became apparent. As the battle heated up, there were many calls to my office during which one side attempted to extract information to use against the other. Each faction attempted to convince anyone who would listen that they were in the right.

There were many accusations. Inevitably, I assume, attorneys got involved. The energy and bitterness of this fight seemed as if it could go on forever. Each time I received a message that one of the many players in this drama had called, my stomach would churn.

I would brace myself for the conversation and cringe as I listened to the cruel words they spoke about and to one another. Everyone took sides, and all sides worked hard to gain my loyalty, as if somehow I had control over this sum of money. They called each other terrible names, which they repeated to me with gusto. When I regularly refused to be drawn into the fighting, they had a few choice names for me as well. They cajoled and joked and yelled, all in an effort to get what they believed was rightfully theirs. Finally, after a few years of fighting, they began to calm down. Perhaps out of sheer exhaustion, they slowly began to let the dust settle.

Ultimately, it was all for nothing. Everyone was obliged to accept the terms spelled out in this despicable trust document. Ronald had prevailed. He had seen these arguments coming and, to some extent, had forged them. He had insured that they would live on, at least for a few years. But how many cruel words were spoken, how many hurtful thoughts were thought? The astonishing thing to my mind was not that the family continued to argue for so long but that the battle was orchestrated from beyond the grave through the means of this legal document.

> Ronald demonstrated his "I'll-Pay-the-Bill-If-You-Just..." attitude from beyond the grave. He had perfected the use of money as a weapon.

What an unfortunate legacy Ronald left with his money. How sad that he didn't see his chance to sow the seeds of peace in his family. Instead, he simply amplified the divisions that already existed, kept his family ground down in their old patterns of battle. This story, however, isn't without a silver lining. As we'll see later in this chapter, his shortsightedness did create an opportunity for one young woman to turn the tide in this unhappy family.

The Emotions of Estate Planning

It seems as if estate planning should be fairly easy. With the help of a qualified estate attorney, you simply create a will or a trust that spells out your wishes. For many people, it really is a fairly straight-forward process. But even with a simple estate and even in a harmonious family, the estate planning process can be quite emotional.

When I worked through my own personal plan, I was quite surprised by how emotional the whole thing was. Although I didn't expect that I would, since I work with these issues regularly, I discovered a fair amount of resistance to thinking about my own death. It wasn't that I pretend I'll never die; it was just that I didn't like contemplating the lives of my children and their children without me there to be a part of it all. I found myself imagining milestones in their lives that I wouldn't want to miss but probably would. Oddly enough, planning for the distribution of my own estate made me feel a bit lonely!

It's not just sentimental types like me who find estate planning emotional. It can also be very challenging for those who hate to give up control. For these people, estate planning is usually approached as a major opportunity to control from beyond the grave. This can be done to a certain degree, but inevitably there will be things that can't be managed. You can dictate many things in a will or a trust, but eventually your heirs will be able to do what they wish with the money or other things they inherit. For many people, especially those who wish to control everything, it can be hard and unpleasant to think about some family members on their own, especially if they don't seem quite ready for independence. It's easy to imagine the mistakes they might make (probably ones we ourselves made!) and know that we won't be able to prevent them.

As we discussed in the last chapter, many people struggle with the issue of leaving money to their children at all. This is a philosophical question that's worthy of serious reflection. Should we give our children a leg up with an inheritance, or is it better for them to earn it all themselves? Will an inheritance improve their lives, or will it make them lazy? Many people remember all the crazy mistakes they've made in their own lives and try to imagine whether or not an inheritance might prevent their kids from making similar mistakes or perhaps contribute to them. Or it may be the opposite: They think about those things they couldn't or didn't do because they simply didn't have enough money and hope an inheritance will give their children greater freedom to explore life. We all hope to spare our kids some of the hardships that we ourselves experienced or to facilitate opportunities we never had.

Obviously this issue of leaving money or not is a very personal one, and we must all make our own decisions about it. But no matter what you decide, it can be worthwhile to consider what might be behind your decision. For example, there are several wealthy people with whom I've worked who have decided not to leave too much of a fortune to their children. In one case, a man with a very peaceful and empowered attitude toward his money did this because he had worked hard for all he had and valued that work experience. He very much wanted that same experience for his children and felt that too much money might dampen their ambitions. It was more important to him that his children be independent and ambitious than it was that they be comfortable financially. While he certainly didn't leave them penniless, he chose to use his estate plan as a way to encourage them to create their own prosperity.

Another wealthy man who made the same decision had a very different motivation. For him, it was about judgment and domination. He had no faith in his own children and felt certain that a sizable inheritance would make them reckless. For him, refusing to leave money to his children was a clear and conscious statement of his distrust. Unfortunately, he wasn't able to see beyond that distrust. His only thoughts were of preserving his money and keeping his children from running through it.

The same decision in each case but very different motivations and hugely different legacies. One father left a message of love and trust; the other, only his disappointment. It's hard to imagine the children of this second man inheriting a healthy relationship to money or considering this act a loving one!

> Identical decisions by two different people reflect opposite attitudes. One grew from a "Spread-the-Joy" approach, the other from a "Money-Is-King" attitude.

Clearly, one of the great opportunities and also one of the hardest parts of this whole estate-planning endeavor is this very subtle self-evaluation. If we give serious thought to these delicate issues, we must inevitably confront ourselves and all that we believe about our money and the people to whom we might leave it. In our estate plan, there will be no hiding. Our beliefs about money and, to some extent, our motivations will be on display. And once our estate plan goes into effect (meaning at our death), there will be no further opportunities to change it. Therefore it behooves us to go about this process with the greatest clarity and the greatest compassion possible.

If the man described above who decided not to leave an inheritance to his children because he didn't trust them had been able to truly reflect on the impact of that message, might he have reconsidered? He believed he was being prudent, a tough-minded, realistic money man. But what if some honest reflection had made him realize that he was also being harsh and that his approach might just be harmful to his children? One can only wonder if he would have acted differently. I'm not saying that he should or should not have left money to his kids; I am saying that his estate plan says as much about him as it does about his children and perhaps more. It may indeed speak of his tough-mindedness, but it also speaks of his disapproval of his family and of his willingness to use money to express it. And those things too are part of his financial legacy.

My goal in telling these stories is to encourage you to think more broadly about your money and especially your emotional relationship to it as you plan your last financial transaction. I believe that we can all be more conscious and aware as we plan the distribution of our estate. We can cast a wider net, express gratitude to those who have been kind to us or forgiveness to those who have not. We can support causes and friends and organizations. We can take steps toward creating peace in our families and in our communities. In short, we can put our money where our hearts have truly been.

Whatever emotion has dominated your financial life will

undoubtedly permeate the estate planning process for you, and so the exercise of writing up a plan is an excellent opportunity to observe and evaluate. It's useful to question your motivation at every turn as you draw up the stipulations that go into your estate documents. For example, is your first tendency to dictate everything that your heirs can and cannot do with their money? Why is that? Is that mostly your fear of losing control or their genuine need of your help? Do you wish to withhold money from your heirs until they reach a certain age? Is that because you believe opportunities will come up for them later in their lives and you want them to have the freedom to explore them? Or is it really because you don't trust their ability to manage it?

Or are you one of those people who refuses to even think about drawing up a will or a trust? There are lots of people who never seem able to get around to this task. If you're one of them, is it because you just really don't care what happens to your money when you're no longer in charge or because the whole issue of death is too hard to contemplate? Or does not taking this important step for the good of your family give you a sense of total control?

Money is the mirror in which we glimpse our true selves.

Obviously it's not my place to say what anyone should or should not do in their own estate plan. It is a highly personal instrument that demands, I believe, a great deal of honesty and introspection. But I have seen some very hurtful plans that leave bad feeling and cause irreparable damage and unnecessary pain. At times, it's the result of malice or anger, but more often it's a simple matter of stumbling blindly through with very little attention to the impact of our words and our deeds.

My sincere hope here is to prompt us all to be more conscious as we consider our money so that we can be deliberate and self-aware as we make our estate decisions. Hopefully from that awareness, we will seize the opportunity estate planning offers to move toward a more peaceful relationship to our money and more responsible actions. Would that we all could grow to have the "Spread-the-Joy" attitude.

An Act of Love

Despite all our reticence about imagining our own death, thinking about our families without us, or planning out the disbursement of our monies, estate planning is still essentially a great act of love. Leaving your financial house in order is a gift to your loved ones. It relieves them of a great deal of uncertainty, work, and confusion. Leaving your financial house in disarray, on the other hand, is irresponsible and a very unkind thing to do to your family. But beyond that obvious gift of sparing your heirs the tedious work that often follows a death when no plans have been made, there's more. The steps we take as we go through this work of organizing an estate can be motivated by great love, and the process can be very personally rewarding. We get to choose what to focus on as we complete this task. The focus can be on ourselves and the end of our life or on the people we love.

When you approach estate planning with a loving mind-set you're bestowing gifts on those you love. These gifts will take them into a phase of their life that you won't be around to see, but at least, through your bequest, you can be a part of it. It focuses far more on the gift and the recipient than it does on death and the giver. The careful arrangement of your financial affairs shows the people you love very clearly that you're thinking of them long into the future.

Although most of us think first about our family, our gifts don't have to stop there. Many people include expressions of love and gratitude for their friends or others who have made an impact on them in their wills and trusts. The gift needn't be large. In fact, it may be just a token. But it bestows a blessing all the same and honors a meaningful relationship.

Why shouldn't our estate planning be at least a little bit fun? It's about giving every bit as much as it is about leaving. It's true that we in the financial services industry haven't approached it too often from this point of view, but why shouldn't we look at it this way? In my opinion, our estate planning should be a conscious act of love.

Getting Down to the Details

Despite all that I say about estate planning being a loving thing to do and personally rewarding, unfortunately it's also quite true that it can be somewhat tedious. There are lots of details to attend to that a trusted estate-planning attorney can help you with, but many people find it a rather laborious task nevertheless.

The reward of this endeavor, however, is not in the doing; the reward is for your family. I've seen many times the sense of relief and satisfaction that people feel when they finally get their estate plan in order. It really is a good feeling to know that you've done all you can to help your children and other heirs get on with their lives after your death.

In my work, I get to see it both ways. I work with families who have everything organized. For them, no matter how emotional the death of the loved one is, at least the financial side of things is clear and relatively easy. The transfer of money from one generation to the next or from one individual to another can be smooth and often quick. This relieves the grieving family members of some of the worry and work.

On the other hand, for families who haven't put their financial house in order, things can be a mess. It can take months and sometimes even years to sort everything out. Often, there are holdings that get forgotten and turn up long after, still in the name of the deceased person. This can be fixed but not without considerable effort. Dividends, interest payments, and sometimes even stock certificates can be lost. More serious still, questions like that of the guardianship for minor children can be very difficult to decide and can end up in the courts. All of this opens the door to arguments within a family where there is money to be divided and no directions for doing so. It takes an especially harmonious family to work it all out.

So where do you begin if you are one of the millions of people without a written plan for what's to happen to your money after you die? Some basic information on estate taxes is as good a place as any to start.

I would say that the financial services industry has approached estate planning primarily from the point of view of taxes. Good estate planning can often reduce an estate-tax bill if there is to be one. Most people want to minimize the best they can the amount of money that's taken from their estate in the form of taxes. Most of us want to see as much go to our families, friends, and charitable interests as possible. So it's a perfectly reasonable and practical concern that often drives the process of estate planning initially.

Currently, under the Economic Growth and Tax Relief Reconciliation Act of 2001, you can pass an estate of $2 million without estate taxes to your children and other heirs. (Generally, no estate taxes apply when passing an estate between spouses.) The amount that can be sheltered from estate tax will increase to $3.5 million by the year 2009. In 2010, the estate tax will disappear for one year. Then, in 2011, as the law stands now, things will change again. Unless there is further legislation passed to alter this, at that point, the maximum amount that can pass estate tax free will revert to $1 million, as it was some time ago. Because the amount of money that can be left without being subject to estate taxes has increased, many people may feel that they no longer need to draw up an estate plan. But, in fact, there is a great deal more to your planning than just avoiding undue taxes.

Just as important to most families are some of the other issues addressed in a thorough plan. A number of them are quite significant. If you own personal property (not money) that's to be passed on, for example, who is to inherit what? At what age are your heirs to inherit their money or possessions? Who is to serve as the guardian to minor children, and how can you provide privacy and simplicity for your family?

Often the weight of these kinds of questions can take a person by surprise. What started out as a tax issue ends up being highly emotional and difficult. The gravity of a decision about who would care for minor children for example can be heavy. There can be arguments about some of these more complex family issues. Sometimes, if couples can't agree, that very disagreement becomes the reason that the whole process is left incomplete.

But if you're ready to dive in, there are some simple steps to follow that will start you on your way to leaving the legacy you wish to leave. Understand first that you will want to work with a legal professional for the drafting and execution of your will and/or your trust. The more complicated your estate or your personal situation, the more important it is that your plan be done correctly. You want to take advantage of current tax law and also shape the document to fit your needs and your wishes. You may also want to meet with your CPA and your financial adviser as you move through this process. Scheduling an appointment with a reputable estate-planning attorney (and allowing yourself plenty of time to prepare for it) is a good first step to get you going. From that point, there are roughly ten other steps you will need to take. Some of these will be carried out in a quiet, soul-searching kind of way. Others are for public viewing.

Once you're ready to begin, you should *draw up an inventory* of your assets and possessions. This is a very useful thing to do not only for your estate plan but also for many other financial situations as well. It's helpful to include not only what you own but also where it's kept or housed and in what name it's held. Do you have financial assets in joint name with your spouse, for example? Do you have IRAs at banks, brokerage firms, insurance companies? Are your retirement funds still with your employer? What about hard assets like jewelry or art? Where are they? Do you own real estate? Whose name is it in and where are the titles?

The next step is to *think about your objectives.* This is one of the creative parts of the plan. To whom do you wish to give your money? Are there special issues in your family—like a person who will need ongoing care or an individual who has already received a portion of his or her inheritance through earlier gifting—that you want to take into account as you make your decisions? Is there a special project you would like to fund, like endowing a chair at a university or making a gift to an organization? Is there something you wish your heirs to do before they receive your money or something you wish to encourage them to do with it? It may be as simple as reaching a certain age or something more complicated, like getting a diploma. This phase of your planning is your chance to think about how you would like to continue to teach with your money and to express your values.

The next step is to *examine and understand the types of tools that are available* to you for the estate plan itself. I refer here to things like a will versus a trust or other legal structures. It isn't within the scope of this book to spell out the many forms of trusts or other entities available or to distinguish the various uses of each one. These are the types of things you must sort out with your attorney, but if you are clear on what you wish to accomplish and on the total inventory of assets that you're working with, he or she can help you sort out which vehicles will work best for your particular set of objectives.

Getting started is half the battle! One you've drawn up an inventory of your assets, sorted out your objectives, and considered what type of plan you may need, it's time to meet with your attorney and *get the appropriate documents in place.* This part of the process requires a bit of work. Documents must be executed, assets must be moved into the proper trust if you're using one, and various financial institutions must be contacted. But once you've done this work, you've come a long way toward getting your financial house in order.

It's very important at this phase that there be diligent follow-through. It's one thing to draw up and execute a trust, for example, but if stocks, bonds, real estate, and the like aren't moved into the name of the trust, it's all been for naught. Make sure you complete all the steps your attorney will spell out for you in completing your plan.

At this point, many people like to compose a *letter of instruction* for their family. This is an expansion of the inventory you've already made. It provides the names of professionals with whom you've worked, any special instructions regarding your funeral, and even biographical information for the person writing your obituary.

Finally it's very important to *prepare for incapacity.* We tend to think of estate planning only in relation to our death. But in our planning, we must also think about a time when we're still alive but no longer able to handle our own affairs. This part of planning may include long-term-care insurance, a clear line of succession in who can make financial and medical decisions on your behalf, a power of attorney, a health-care proxy, and a living will. Through all of these, you're not only protecting your family but also clearly expressing your wishes. You're offering them guidance even as you're granting them authority.

As you're getting your financial house in order in this very productive way, it's also a good idea to *give special attention to your beneficiaries.* There are several types of accounts that require you to state specific beneficiaries. These include retirement accounts as well as several other types of investment products. At your death, these monies pass directly to the person, persons, or entities you have named. For some people, these accounts represent very substantial portions of their estate. Therefore, it's important to be mindful of your beneficiary designations and to revisit them from time to time. They can and should be updated on a regular basis. If people fail to review their beneficiaries periodically, it's not at all uncommon to find a deceased person still listed as a beneficiary at the time of your death or even an ex-spouse. You can imagine the types of problems this can cause within a family.

Many people simply list their spouse as primary beneficiary and then neglect to list a contingent or secondary recipient, but it's always good to list contingent beneficiaries as well. Your spouse may predecease you. The two of you may die together. With no secondary beneficiary listed, the monies would simply pour into your estate and, perhaps, increase the tax on it. If you have a contingent beneficiary listed and the primary beneficiary cannot receive the assets for some reason, they will move automatically to that second person or persons whom you have named.

Finally, many people wish to list their trust as a beneficiary, and this is certainly acceptable. However, it's a tricky matter requiring a little extra work. If this is what you wish to do, be sure to consult your attorney to be certain that everything is correctly set up.

If you have discovered throughout this whole process that you would really like to give some money away, there are some *gifting strategies* that you should discuss with your lawyer, your CPA, and also your financial adviser. In my experience, few people give significant gifts for the tax benefits alone. But combine those benefits with a philanthropic heart, and you might find that you lean in that direction. If you do, there are a number of very effective strategies that your tax professional can describe that will help others through a generous gift and potentially help your family through reduced taxation.

It's very important that the person you choose to be *executor of your will or the successor trustee on your trust* be willing and able. It's a good idea to talk things over with this person or these people ahead of time to be sure that they'll be able to handle your affairs in a timely and competent way and also that they understand the responsibility they're assuming. This is an important job. Both you and/or your family may be dependent on them. Look for family members or friends or even professionals whom you trust to have your family's best interests in mind at all times, someone who can navigate the bureaucracy that he or she will inevitably be involved in, and someone who has the time to do this work.

It may seem that once you've gotten this far, your work is done. And for the time being, it is. But *all of these documents must be periodically reviewed.* Obviously you need to revisit things if there's been a major change in your life, like a divorce or a death. In addition, you should review your estate plan if there has been a shift in your financial life, like a windfall of some sort, the sale of business, or an inheritance. And there are other things that can make you revise your plan as well, like a significant change in the tax laws, for example, that require you to rethink your strategy. In any case, I suggest that you review your estate documents every couple of years to verify that everything is still the way you want it to be and that the plan you've put in place still expresses your highest priorities.

Clearly drawing up an effective estate plan takes some work, but it's vital if you wish to take care of your family as well as your money after your death. It's more than just a gift to your family; it's also a statement of who you were in relation to your money. It's your last and perhaps most telling opportunity to put your money where your heart is, your last chance to let your money speak for you.

A Peace Treaty at Last

Even a badly conceived estate plan can have an unexpected happy ending. And I'm happy to report that this was the case with my client Ronald, who stirred up such turmoil in his family through his mean-spirited trust. It was he who created a trust document that galvanized his family and pushed them into years of battle over the money that he left.

His story would seem only sad and negative if it weren't for the actions of one family member, a young woman who first called a halt to the arguing. It was she who finally stood up and said, "Enough!" Slowly, they began to resolve their differences. Perhaps, in the scheme of things, what Ronald did manage to do was to give this young woman an opportunity to step into her own role of peacemaker in this family. I would like to believe that, on a spiritual level, this was their agreement: that, given the long history of family fighting, he would set the stage for her to fulfill a potential that she developed through this battle. Because of the fighting in her family, she grew to be a leader and a peacemaker.

Even in this unhappy story, there was an example of greatness. She recognized that she was being offered a vital opportunity to grow, and she didn't shrink from it. Because she was able to see beyond the fighting and because she had a mature and peaceful relationship to money, she didn't refuse to shoulder the difficult responsibility of breaking the cycle of argument within this group. And it's to the credit of the other family members that they accepted her leadership. Perhaps for her to become the peace-maker that she truly was, things had to play out as they did. It's not always easy to understand the meaning of events or actions. Sometimes it takes more than one generation for a story to unfold and the legacy it represents to be revealed.

An "All-Is-Well" attitude to money can end even the worst of battles.

Final Thoughts

How fortunate we all are to live in this time when money is moving in our country like never before. What an opportunity! And yet how easy it would be for this great migration of wealth to go unnoticed. As we all participate in whatever small or perhaps large ways are available to us, the simple route would be to change nothing, to afford money power and significance in our lives without ever really examining what it means or who we are in relation to it. But as I have stressed throughout *The Value of Money*, there is great power and potential in that examination.

The financial circumstances of our day are inviting us to become aware and to evaluate our belief systems around money, to go well beyond simply contemplating how we spend it or how much we need or want. They invite us to engage with our money in more creative ways than we have done in the past, to take the measure of ourselves in our dealing with it, and to put it to constructive use in all areas of our life.

To my mind, no role that money plays in our life is greater than its functions as mirror to our inner self and bridge to our material world. The most inspiring stories I've seen in my years of advising on financial matters have been those in which my clients have seized the opportunities that money has presented for growth, change, and self-awareness. The greatest financial peace I have witnessed has grown out of this awareness and from the creative and relaxed relationship to money it promotes. It's these individuals who lead the way in what could be a radical change in our attitude toward money. If all of us could begin to accept the many invitations for self-scrutiny that money offers us and become more aware and more proactive in our relationship to it, I feel real hope for financial peace for us all.

No matter what you may feel your own personal financial status in our world is, no matter how satisfied or dissatisfied you may be, there's no denying that we in the United States enjoy great prosperity. We all control money to some extent. We all make decisions on it. And although many of us may feel that we lack money, although we may have concerns and fears, we still enjoy the freedoms that money can provide at least to some degree. Our culture has focused with intensity on money—creating wealth and a standard of living for the majority that would be unimaginable in many other parts of the world. And while there has certainly been excess and harm in that expansion, it has been largely beneficial.

And yet how little we have focused on the soulful side of money. How little we have attended to our complex relationship to this cornerstone of our lives and of our society. Even as we have pursued wealth itself, we have failed to cultivate awareness and a mindful use of this most basic and powerful tool, our money.

But the circumstances of our time are inviting us to do just that. Now more than ever, we have an opportunity to use money, not only to fulfill our personal dreams but also to explore our own beings.

Through the prism of money, we can observe our behavior, our relationship to others, our beliefs about ourselves, our sense of our place in the world. We can compare the person we really want to be to the person we really are. And if those two are far apart, we can begin to bring them together. Our money becomes a part of that process, too.

Throughout *The Value of Money* I have tried to show ways in which we can all tackle, from both the financial and the emotional angles, the challenging money situations that arise in our lives. I have hoped throughout to offer ideas that will ease some of the money fears I have observed, not only in my clients but also in myself. My hope has been to give you confidence as you enter the inevitable transitions of normal life with all of their emotional and financial complications.

But to my mind, that confidence is only the first step to a truly peaceful and joyful relationship to money. It opens the door to the real power of money in our lives—its potential to illuminate our inner lives, then to assist us as we try to express our best selves in the world. This is the greatest gift that money has to offer us, its greatest role.

How is it that you wish to be in relationship to your money? What is it that you want your money to say about you? If you could show your purest, most beautiful self to the world, what would that person look like? What part can your money play in that presentation?

These are the types of questions I hope we will all ask ourselves as we enter into this period of "money in motion."

For myself, I seek peace. I seek the joy of generosity and compassion, the calm of believing there are enough resources in the world for all of us. And I want that peace for others as well. I want everyone to feel such comfort with the money in their lives that they share more easily, worry less, and enjoy more. I want all of us to recognize our bad behaviors around money and laugh at ourselves as we gracefully change. I want us to understand that money is a only a tool and that it doesn't make us happy even as we recognize that handling it with responsibility, generosity, and joy certainly can. I want us all to unclench our hearts when it comes to our money, care about it less even as we care for it more. I want us to approach it with grace and ease. Such an attitude will create abundance in our lives, no matter what our financial status is, no matter what stage of life we are in.

This is the invitation I believe the massive shift of wealth offers to each and every one of us, an invitation to elevate our attitudes, beliefs, and habits around money. I hope and pray that this is something we will all accept.

BOOKS OF INTEREST

Bach, David. *The Automatic Millionaire: A Powerful One-Step Plan to Live and Finish Rich.* New York: Broadway Books, 2004.

Bryan, Mark, and Julia Cameron. *Money Drunk, Money Sober: 90 Days to Financial Freedom.* New York: The Ballantine Publishing Group, 1992.

Chatzky, Jean. *You Don't Have to Be Rich: Comfort, Happiness, and Financial Security on Your Own Terms.* New York: The Penguin Group, 2003.

Cohen, Alan. *Relax Into Wealth: How to Get More by Doing Less.* New York: Jeremy P. Tarcher, 2006.

Eisenberg, Lee. *The Number: What Do You Need for the Rest of Your Life and What Will It Cost?* New York: Free Press, 2006.

Kinder, George. *The Seven Stages of Money Maturity: Understanding the Spirit and Value of Money in Your Life.* New York: Dell Publishing, 1999.

Kiyosaki, Robert T., and Sharon L. Lechter. *Rich Dad, Poor Dad: What the Rich Teach Their Kids About Money—That the Poor and Middle Class Do Not!* New York: Time Warner Paperbacks, 2002.

Kulananda and Dominic Houlder. *Mindfulness and Money: The Buddhist Path of Abundance.* New York: Broadway Books, 2002.

Needleman, Jacob. *Money and the Meaning of Life.* New York: Doubleday, 1991.

Needleman, Jacob, et al. *Money, Money, Money: The Search for Wealth and the Pursuit of Happiness.* Carlsbad, CA: Hay House, 1998.

Offill, Jenny, and Elissa Schappell, editors. *Money Changes Everything: Twenty-two Writers Tackle the Last Taboo with Tales of Sudden Windfalls, Staggering Debts, and Other Surprising Turns of Fortune.* New York: Doubleday, 2007.

Orman, Suze. *The 9 Steps to Financial Freedom: Practical and Spiritual Steps So You Can Stop Worrying.* New York: Three Rivers Press, 1997, 2000.

Perle, Liz. *Money, A Memoir: Women, Emotions and Cash.* New York: Henry Holt and Co., 2006.

Ramsey, Dave. *The Total Money Makeover: A Proven Plan for Financial Fitness.* Nashville, Tennessee: Thomas Nelson, Inc., 2007.

Stanny, Barbara. *Prince Charming Isn't Coming: How Women Get Smart about Money.* New York: Viking Penguin, 1997.

Stav, Julie. *The Money in You!: Discover Your Financial Personality and Live the Millionaire's Life*. New York: HarperCollins, 2007.

Williams, Rosemary, with Joanne Kabak. *The Woman's Book of Money and Spiritual Vision: Putting Your Spiritual Values into Financial Practice*. Maui, Hawaii: Inner Ocean Publishing, Inc., 2001.

ACKNOWLEDGMENTS

I would like to express my gratitude to the many people who have inspired and supported me throughout the writing of this book.

I'm thankful first and foremost to all my clients who have shared their stories and opened their financial lives to me for these last twenty-five years. I'm truly humbled by the confidence that you place in all of us each and every day and honored to play a role in your lives.

I'm grateful as well to my business partner, Greg Hall, and our assistant, Linda Parker. I couldn't imagine a finer or more caring team to work with, or for that matter, a more fun group. May our business lives always be as enjoyable as they have become over the last few years.

My thanks to Don Stillman for his belief in this message, and to both Kevin McAfee and Randy Smith for their early encouragement and wise counsel.

Thank you to publisher Joel Fotinos of Tarcher/Penguin for working with me as the message of *The Value of Money* took shape and for your guidance and honesty. I'm immensely grateful as well to editor Sara Carder for your objective readings and thoughtful suggestions. And thank you, Kat Obertance, for being a steady and reliable go-between and always there ready to help.

To my friends, Les Chochottes, thank you for moral support, constant seeking, and great fun. Sara, Rachel, Teri, Mylene, Carol, and Denise—you're a wonderful group of women and I'm lucky to know you. And gratitude as well to JoAnn Vandenberg Hunt and to Kathy Gilman for your constant support, wisdom, and encouragement.

Deep gratitude to my dear late friend Starla Drum. There's no one with whom I've shared more money experiences than you. I so wish I could also share this book with you now.

To my parents, John and Margaret McCarthy, thanks for all those years of good example on the ins and outs of money management.

I'm honored to be the mother of the best kids ever—Veronica and Michael. You have always believed in my work and always encouraged me. Thank you.

And lastly to my DKS, as so many times before, I bow down in gratitude.

GLOSSARY

Beneficiary: An individual, institution, or estate that receives or may become eligible to receive benefits under any number of different types of contracts.

Bond: A debt instrument in which an investor loans money to an entity (corporate or governmental) that borrows the funds for a defined period of time at a fixed interest rate. Bonds are used by companies, municipalities, states, and U.S. and foreign governments to finance a variety of projects and activities.

Diversification: An investment strategy designed to reduce exposure to risk by combining a variety of different types of investments.

Estate: All assets owned by an individual at death to be distributed to heirs.

Estate Planning: The preparation of a plan of administration and disposition of one's property before or after death.

Growth: An investing strategy or concept whereby a security will appreciate in value over a period of time.

Individual Retirement Account (IRA): A retirement account for individuals that permits them to set aside money each year with earnings tax-deferred until withdrawal at age 59½ or later (or earlier with a penalty).

Stock: A type of security that signifies ownership and represents a claim on part of the corporation's assets and earnings. Also known as "shares" or "equity."

Trust: A legal arrangement in which an individual gives fiduciary control of property to a person or institution (the trustee) for the benefit of beneficiaries.

401(k): A retirement plan offered by a corporation to its employees to set aside tax-deferred income for retirement purposes. The name 401(k) comes from the IRS section describing the program.

403(b): A retirement plan similar to a 401(k) but offered by nonprofit organizations instead of corporations. Employees are permitted to make tax-deferred contributions for retirement purposes.

INDEX

Susan McCarthy began her career as a college professor teaching French language and literature. In 1984, she left academic circles for the business world. After twenty-three years with Morgan Stanley (and its predecessors), she recently joined Wachovia Securities as a First Vice President and Financial Adviser. She and her team specialize in working with individuals and institutions, designing, implementing, and monitoring investment portfolios to meet a variety of needs.

Susan lives with her two children in Oklahoma City.